Essential Teaching Skills

Chris Kyriacou

SIMON & SCHUSTER
EDUCATION

© Chris Kyriacou 1991

First published in 1991 by
Basil Blackwell Ltd

Reprinted 1991, 1992 (twice), 1993 (twice), 1994

Third and subsequent impressions published by
Simon and Schuster Education
Campus 400
Maylands Avenue
Hemel Hempstead HP2 7EZ

A catalogue record for this book is available from the British Library

ISBN 0-7501-0369-8

Printed and bound by T. J. Press, Padstow

Cartoons by Nick Davies

Thanks to Steven Gill of Cardinal
Newman Middle School, Oxford,
for the cover illustration

Contents

For Christine and Helen

Preface

In my book *Effective Teaching in Schools* (Kyriacou, 1986a), I described effective teaching as essentially setting up a learning activity (or task or experience) that successfully brings about the type of pupil learning (knowledge, understanding, skills and attitudes) that is intended by the teacher. I argued that for this to occur, the teaching needs to fulfil three conditions:

- it elicits and sustains pupils' attention to the learning activity
- it elicits and sustains pupils' motivation and effort to learn from the learning activity
- the learning activity is appropriate for the type of pupil learning you wish to bring about.

In this book, I outline the teaching skills which are involved in effective teaching. The book is designed to meet the needs of student teachers and experienced teachers wishing to explore and develop their own practice, and will also be of use to those involved in helping others to develop teaching skills or with an interest in the topic generally.

1 Developing your teaching skills

The essence of being an effective teacher lies in knowing what to do to foster pupils' learning and being able to do it. Effective teaching is primarily concerned with setting up a learning activity for each pupil which is successful in bringing about the type of learning the teacher intends. The difference between knowing what to do and being able to do it can be well-illustrated by making an analogy with playing tennis. A player may know that in a particular situation a lob over the opponent's head is required, but whether that shot can be played successfully may be an entirely different matter! The player's skills operate in two ways here. First, the decision-making skill involved in deciding that a lob is in fact the most appropriate shot required; second, the action skill involved in executing that shot.

The nature of teaching skills

You must develop your action skills

The art of successful teaching is thus crucially bound up with developing both decision-making skills and action skills. This distinction between these two types of skills is extremely important, because teaching is as much a thinking activity as it is observable actions. Developing your skills as a teacher therefore is as much about developing and extending the type of decisions you make about your own teaching as it is about the successful execution of those decisions.

Almost all teachers during their initial training will spend some time observing experienced teachers, and increasing numbers of experienced teachers now spend some time observing colleagues as part of their own or their colleagues' programme of professional development. Such observation can be immensely valuable; seeing how another teacher performs can stimulate your own ideas about your teaching. It may do this simply by acting as a model, either good or bad (seeing a colleague use an exceptionally well-prepared worksheet or one containing some obvious shortcomings may both stimulate your thinking about your own use of worksheets). Equally well, and more frequently, observation is stimulating because of the creative tension caused by trying to match your own decision-making about teaching with the decisions you infer your colleague has made. For example, you may normally go over some key points regarding why an experimental design used might be suspect, with the class as a whole, only to see a colleague using small-group discussion instead. As a result, you may be stimulated to think about the reasons for this. Indeed, the benefits of classroom observation are greatly enhanced by having some time available before and after the lesson for discussion about the teaching.

The features of teaching skills
Over the years much has been written about classroom teaching skills. The impetus for this has included those concerned with the initial training and in-service training of teachers, those concerned to monitor the standard and quality of teaching performance, those involved in schemes of teacher appraisal, and those concerned with understanding, as a research endeavour, what constitutes successful teaching. As such, there is now a massive literature available for study.

The nature of teaching skills has received much attention. Calderhead (1986) has suggested that it is useful to define teaching skills in terms of a number of features:

- they are intended to achieve a particular goal
- they take account of the particular context
- they require precision and fine-tuning
- they are performed smoothly
- they are acquired through training and practice.

Studies of teaching skills

A particularly interesting study of teaching skills has been reported by Tomlinson and Smith (1985), who have developed a technique called radio-assisted practice (RAP). This enables teacher trainers to communicate directly with student teachers during a lesson they are observing, using miniaturised radio microphones and receivers. As a result, the trainer is able to offer advice and guidance while the lesson is in progress, and when the student teacher is in the thick of decision-making. This approach has highlighted the need for the trainer and the student teacher to share a clear and explicit understanding of key teaching skills, so that a single word can be used to communicate important guidance during RAP. Essentially, Tomlinson and Smith see teaching skills as purposeful activities which enable teachers to achieve their goals. Such skills are executed with ease, speed and smoothness.

Another study aimed at developing teaching skills in student teachers was the Teacher Education Project. This was based on over 1000 lesson observations and over 200 interviews with student teachers and experienced teachers (Wragg, 1984). Wragg sees teaching skills as strategies that teachers use which facilitate pupils learning something worthwhile and which are acknowledged by those competent to judge as being skills. Wragg also argues that the skill should be capable of being repeated. He further points out that focusing on particular skills in isolation can be unhelpful because they can become less meaningful out of context. Wragg believes that it is better to analyse particular skills in relation to broad areas of activity. The Teacher Education Project did this by looking at class management, mixed-ability teaching, questioning and explaining.

Teachers' thinking

As well as studies focusing on developing skills amongst student teachers, a number of writers have focused on studying what experienced teachers think about the skills they use in teaching.

Leinhardt and Greeno (1986), for example, argue that teaching is a complex cognitive skill based on knowledge about how to construct and conduct a lesson, and knowledge about the content to be taught. This skill enables the teacher to construct plans and make rapid decisions in the light of changing circumstances. They argue that experienced teachers develop sets of organised actions which they can apply flexibly and with little mental effort in appropriate situations. Calderhead (1986) explains this well by using the analogy of going to a restaurant. Once you have been to several types of restaurant, you develop knowledge about the procedures that generally operate:

whether you find a table or are shown to one, how you order from a menu, and when and how you pay. Such experience enables you to go to a new restaurant and cope with getting what you want reasonably skilfully. For someone who has never been to a restaurant, few sets of organised actions have been built up. For all the person may know, you may have to go to the kitchen, select some meat, and cook it yourself! Similarly, experienced teachers have a ready recourse to an appropriate set of behaviours from which to select that behaviour most appropriate to the immediate demands of the situation, whether it is dealing with a pupil who is unable to answer a question posed or noticing a pupil looking out of the window and day-dreaming. Indeed, the reason why teaching is so demanding in the early years is because the new teacher has to build up the expertise of knowing what to do and be able to do it.

A number of writers have pointed out that a particular feature of teaching skills is their interactive nature. The teacher's actions during a lesson continuously need to take account of changing circumstances, many of which can be largely unexpected. Indeed, Clark and Peterson (1986) have noted how teachers' effectiveness in the classroom seems to, in part, depend on how well they modify and change their actions and strategies in the light of how the lesson is going. In this sense, teaching is more like driving which involves negotiating a series of busy roundabouts than it is like driving along a quiet motorway. Clark and Peterson argue that with experience much of this interactive decision-making becomes routine and only partly conscious, so that the teacher only needs to think consciously about circumstances which are more unexpected, unique or require particular attention and care. For the less experienced teacher, much less of the decision-making has become routine and hence there is more to think about while the lesson is in progress.

Teachers' knowledge about teaching

Another important feature of teaching skills is that they clearly draw upon the teachers' knowledge about effective teaching. Shulman (1987) has argued that at the very least this knowledge base includes:

- knowledge about content
- knowledge about broad principles and strategies of classroom management and organisation
- knowledge about curriculum materials and programmes
- knowledge about the teaching of particular content topics
- knowledge about pupils
- knowledge about educational contexts, ranging from the class-room group to aspects of the community
- knowledge about educational aims and values.

For Shulman, teaching skills are bound up with teachers' thinking which draws upon their knowledge base as a basis for judgement and action.

This notion that as much emphasis in considering teaching skills must be given to the knowledge base as to the decision-making process, may seem odd since clearly all decision-making must draw on teachers' knowledge about teaching. The basic point here is that such knowledge is largely implicit and taken for granted. However, if one is concerned with how teachers develop their teaching skills, this knowledge base needs to be made explicit. A commonly used way of doing this is to show teachers a video of their teaching and probe their thinking about what they did and why through this 'stimulated recall' method. This approach essentially tries to re-create the teachers' thinking in process while they were actually teaching (often referred to as 'reflection-in-action').

Yinger (1986), however, has argued that we need to go beyond the use of stimulated-recall techniques to probe more deeply into the teacher's knowledge base. He suggests that a mixture of other methods can be used, such as more sensitive approaches to classroom observation, an analysis of how teachers undertake particular tasks, and in-depth interviews. Yinger argues that such an approach would provide a more sophisticated and realistic conception of the teacher's knowledge base, how it is used as a basis for action, and how it is developed and modified in the light of experience. Results from studies using such a multi-method approach to explore teachers' thinking have been promising (eg Angulo, 1988).

Defining essential teaching skills

Teaching skills can be defined as discrete and coherent activities by teachers which foster pupil learning. In the light of our consideration of teaching skills so far in this chapter, three important elements of teaching skills are discernable.

1 *Knowledge*, comprising the teacher's knowledge about the subject, pupils, curriculum, teaching methods, the influence on teaching and learning of other factors, and knowledge about one's own teaching skills.
2 *Decision-making*, comprising the thinking and decision-making which occurs before, during and after a lesson, concerning how best to achieve the educational outcomes intended.
3 *Action*, comprising the overt behaviour by teachers undertaken to foster pupil learning.

An over-riding feature of teaching skills is that they are purposeful and goal-directed activities which are essentially problem-solving. At its broadest, the problem is how best to deliver effectively the educational outcomes, in terms of pupil learning, required. More specifically, teaching skills are concerned with all the short-term and immediate problems faced before, during and after the lesson, such as 'How can I lay out the key points on a topic on a single overhead transparency?', 'How can I signal to a pupil to stop talking without interrupting what I am explaining to the whole class?', 'What can I write when assessing a piece of pupils' work to highlight a flaw in the pupil's argument?'.

Teaching skills are also concerned with the long-term problems of effective teaching, such as 'Which textbook series best meets the needs of my pupils?', 'How best can I update my subject matter knowledge?', 'How do I best prepare pupils for the work they will be doing in future years?'.

Identifying essential teaching skills

One of the major problems in trying to identify a list of essential teaching skills is that teaching skills vary from very broad and general skills, such as the planning of lessons, to very specific skills, such as the appropriate length of time to wait for a pupil to answer a question in a particular type of situation. Overall, in considering teaching skills, it seems to be most useful to focus on fairly broad and general skills which are meaningful to teachers and relate to how they think about their teaching. More specific skills can then be discussed as and when they help illustrate and illuminate how these general skills operate. Nevertheless, given the nature of teaching, it is clear that whatever set of general teaching skills is chosen to focus on, the overlap and inter-play between them will be marked, and a good case can always be made by others for focusing on a different set.

Fortunately, over the years there has been a wealth of writing about and use of lists of essential teaching skills, both by those involved in teacher education and by educational researchers. A consideration of such writing indicates that a fairly typical list of the essential teaching skills can be identified. For example, Child (1986), in his analysis of teaching, focuses on knowledge about subject matter and pupils, preparation and planning, the organisation of learning (getting a lesson started, exposition, keeping the lesson going, reinforcement and rounding the lesson off), classroom management (exercising control and discipline), the assessment of pupils' learning and the evaluation of one's own teaching. Similarly, Perrott (1982) focuses on planning, presentation, questions and classroom discussion, affective communication and class organisation. Waterhouse (1983) focuses on classroom appearance, planning and preparation, resources, the teacher as leader and presenter, pupils' motivation and needs, the classroom system, personal relationships, the management of time, management and control, and the intellectual level of activities.

Teacher appraisal

Again, if we look at the wealth of writing dealing with the appraisal of established teachers, the conceptual maps of teaching skills offered largely reflect those already considered. For example, Wragg (1988) offers the following areas for report on a teacher appraisal form: preparation and planning, class management, communication skills (questioning, explaining, etc), pupils' work (appropriate to age and ability, and quality and degree of purpose), assessment of pupils' work and record keeping, knowledge of relevant subject matter and relationships with pupils.

Similarly, the Suffolk Education Department's study of teacher appraisal (Suffolk Education Department, 1987) offers a teacher appraisal profile drawn from the ACAS report of 1986, which comprises:

- *planning and preparation* (eg selects short-term objectives related to the school's curriculum guidelines; is aware of and uses, as and when appropriate, a variety of equipment and resources)
- *classroom organisation and management* (eg uses time and space to maximum advantage; ensures smooth transitions from one activity to another)
- *teaching skills* (eg uses a variety of questioning strategies; has appropriate expectations of children)
- *relationships* (eg shows genuine interest in, and respect for children's words and thoughts; focuses on children's behaviour rather than personality).

Qualities looked for by Her Majesty's Inspectorate (HMI)

In a study which explored the quality of teaching by probationary teachers, the HMI (1988b) observed 861 lessons, of which 504 were in secondary schools and 357 in primary and middle schools. Overall, they graded six per cent of the lessons as excellent, 31 per cent as good, 37 per cent as satisfactory, and 25 per cent as less than satisfactory or worse. The categories they employed to assess the probationers' teaching skills were planning and preparation, classroom organisation, match of work to pupils, classroom interaction and mastery of subject.

It is evident from the reports based on the HMI's inspections of schools that these categories are also used in their assessment of teaching by established teachers and in their advocacy of what constitutes good practice. Interestingly, in their report based on nearly 15 000 lessons in secondary schools (HMI, 1988a), they assessed about two-thirds of the work as satisfactory or better. This is a slightly lower proportion than for the probationary teachers, even though they explicitly state that in assessing the lessons given by probationers, no allowance was made for their inexperience! This would indicate probationers gave slightly better lessons than established teachers. However, we need to be very cautious about what conclusions to draw. In particular, it is worth noting that in one sense such figures are meaningless, since the proportion of lessons assessed as unsatisfactory merely reflect a standard below average. There is no absolute standard of what constitutes a satisfactory lesson. If all lessons improved overnight, the average would be raised, but the proportion assessed as unsatisfactory would almost certainly be about the same. What is meaningful and useful, however, are the characteristics which the HMI highlight as differentiating the good and excellent lessons from the unsatisfactory and poor, and the teaching skills required to achieve the former.

While there is no blueprint for the perfect lesson, the HMI have clearly expressed certain preferences (eg HMI, 1985, 1987, 1990):

- lessons should be purposeful with high expectations conveyed
- pupils should be given some opportunities to organise their own work (over-direction by teachers needs to be guarded against)
- lessons should elicit and sustain pupils' interest, and be perceived by pupils as relevant and challenging
- the work should be well-matched to pupils' abilities and learning needs
- pupils' language should be developed and extended (teachers' questioning skills play a part here)
- a variety of learning activities should be employed
- good order and control should be largely based on skilful management of pupils' involvement in the lesson and mutual respect.

A list of essential teaching skills

Overall, the essential teaching skills involved in contributing to successful classroom practice can be identified and described as follows.

1 *Planning and preparation*: the skills involved in selecting the educational aims and learning outcomes intended for a lesson and how best to achieve these.
2 *Lesson presentation*: the skills involved in successfully engaging pupils in the learning experience, particularly in relation to the quality of instruction.
3 *Lesson management*: the skills involved in managing and organising the learning activities taking place during the lesson to maintain pupils' attention, interest and involvement.
4 *Classroom climate*: the skills involved in establishing and

maintaining positive attitudes and motivation by pupils towards
the lesson.

5 *Discipline*: the skills involved in maintaining good order and
dealing with any pupil misbehaviour which occurs.

6 *Assessing pupils' progress*: the skills involved in assessing
pupils' progress, covering both formative (*viz* intended to aid
pupils' further development) and summative (*viz* providing a
record of attainment) purposes of assessment.

7 *Reflection and evaluation*: the skills involved in evaluating one's
own current teaching practice in order to improve future practice.

These seven sets of essential teaching skills are further developed in
Table 1 (see pp. 10–11) and form the basis for each of the following
chapters of this book.

Two important points, however, need to be borne in mind when
considering these skills. First, there is clearly an interplay between these
seven areas, so that the skills exercised in one area may simultaneously
contribute to another area. For example, smooth transitions between
activities is included within lesson management, but at the same time
will also contribute to maintaining discipline. Second, all the skills
involved in lesson presentation, lesson management, classroom climate
and discipline, are interactive skills. In other words, exercising these
skills involves monitoring, adjusting and responding to what pupils are
doing. Unlike acting on a stage where one can perform without an
audience, these skills cannot be displayed in isolation from their interaction with pupils' behaviour. Even when giving an explanation, for
example, a teacher would, at the very least, be attentive to the faces of
the pupils to judge whether it was being pitched appropriately for their
needs, and might elaborate, alter the pace of delivery, tone of voice,
content, or even stop and ask a question, in the light of what the facial
expressions indicated.

The development of teaching skills

In defining teaching skills earlier, three elements were highlighted: knowledge, decision-making and action. Almost all intending teachers will
have had much experience of being taught as pupils themselves in a
school. Without doubt, this will be the single most important influence
on their knowledge about teaching and the models they have of how to
conduct a lesson.

Numerous studies, however, have indicated just how inadequate
a base this is for attempting to teach one's first few lessons. Long

Table 1 Essential teaching skills.

Planning and preparation
- the lesson plan has clear and suitable aims and objectives
- the content, methods and structure of the lesson selected is appropriate for the pupil learning intended
- the lesson is planned to link up appropriately with past and future lessons
- materials, resources and aids are well-prepared and checked in good time
- all planning decisions take account of the pupils and the context
- the lesson is designed to elicit and sustain pupils' attention, interest and involvement

---

Lesson presentation
- the teacher's manner is confident, relaxed, self-assured, purposeful, and generates interest in the lesson
- the teacher's instructions and explanations are clear and matched to pupils' needs
- the teacher's questions include a variety of types and range and are distributed widely
- a variety of appropriate learning activities are used to foster pupil learning
- pupils are actively involved in the lesson and are given opportunities to organise their own work
- the teacher shows respect and encouragement for pupils' ideas and contributions, and fosters their development
- the work undertaken by pupils is well-matched to their needs
- materials, resources and aids are used to good effect

Lesson management
- the beginning of the lesson is smooth and prompt, and sets up a positive mental set for what is to follow
- pupils' attention, interest and involvement in the lesson is maintained
- pupils' progress during the lesson is carefully monitored
- constructive and helpful feedback is given to pupils to encourage further progress
- transitions between activities are smooth
- the time spent on different activities is well-managed
- the pace and flow of the lesson is adjusted and maintained at an appropriate level throughout the lesson
- adjustments to the lesson plan are made whenever appropriate
- the endings of lesson are used to good effect

Classroom climate
- the climate is purposeful, task-oriented, relaxed, and with an established sense of order
- pupils are supported and encouraged to learn, with high positive expectations conveyed by the teacher
- teacher-pupil relationships are largely based on mutual respect and rapport

- feedback from the teacher contributes to fostering pupil self-confidence and self-esteem
- the appearance and layout of the class is conducive to positive pupil attitudes towards the lesson and facilitates the activities taking place

Discipline
- good order is largely based on the positive classroom climate established and by good lesson presentation and management
- the teacher's authority is established and accepted by pupils
- clear rules and expectations regarding pupil behaviour are conveyed by the teacher at appropriate times
- pupil behaviour is carefully monitored and appropriate actions by the teacher are taken to pre-empt misbehaviour occurring
- pupil misbehaviour is dealt with by an appropriate use of investigation, counselling, academic help, reprimands and punishments
- confrontations are avoided, and skilfully defused

Assessing pupils' progress
- marking of pupils' work during and after lessons is thorough and constructive, and returned in good time
- feedback on assessments is aimed not only to be diagnostic and corrective, but also to encourage further effort and maintain self-confidence, which involves follow-up comments, help or work with particular pupils as appropriate
- a variety of assessment tasks are used, covering both formative and summative purposes
- a variety of records of progress are kept
- some opportunities are given to foster pupils' own assessments of their work and progress
- assessment of pupils' work is used to identify areas of common difficulties, the effectiveness of the teaching, and whether a firm basis for further progress has been established
- assessment is made of the study skills and learning strategies employed by pupils in order to foster their further development

Reflection and evaluation
- lessons are evaluated to inform future planning and practice
- current practice is regularly considered with a view to identifying aspects for useful development
- use is made of a variety of ways to reflect upon and evaluate current practice
- the teacher regularly reviews whether his or her time and effort can be organised to better effect
- the teacher regularly reviews the strategies and techniques he or she uses to deal with sources of stress

experience of being taught certainly provides a broad framework for thinking about how to teach, but once the teacher's role is taken on, it becomes very evident that a whole range of teaching skills needs to be developed. For example, Vonk (1983) asked 21 beginning teachers to keep a diary of their experiences and also asked their pupils to complete a questionnaire about the beginning teachers' teaching skills. Common problems identified included not knowing what to do when, having given an explanation, the pupil did not understand, other than repeating the same explanation; not knowing how to cope with pupils working at different rates, ranging from those who finish early to those making little progress; not knowing which curriculum elements require more attention and emphasis in teaching; and not knowing what to do with pupils they could not control.

Some studies have explicitly compared beginning teachers (either student teachers or probationary teachers) with experienced teachers to highlight the development of teaching skills. Wragg and Wood (1984), for example, noted that student teachers more often became engrossed in private exchanges with pupils so as to lose overall perception of what was going on elsewhere. Experienced teachers, on the other hand, were more able to split their attention between the pupil and the rest of the class, and could break off and comment on what was happening elsewhere, as and when appropriate. Berliner (1987) gave a series of simulated teaching tasks, such as planning a lesson, to three groups: a group of experienced teachers, a group of student teachers, and a group of students intending to train to teach. In the planning task, for example, the experienced teachers were much more selective in using the information provided, preferring to rely on their knowledge of what they could typically expect from pupils of the age and class size given. In effect, the experienced teachers were able to use their repertoire of how to set up and deliver learning activities which is largely denied or non-existent for the other two groups.

Monitoring your own teaching

Another source of information about how teaching skills develop concerns the efforts of experienced teachers to monitor and develop their own skills or to assist with developing those of their colleagues. Such work has taken place either as part of formal schemes of teacher appraisal and staff development (Turner and Clift, 1988) or simply as part of the teacher's own concern to monitor and develop their own practice.

Of particular interest, as an example of the latter, has been the growth of teacher action research (Hustler *et al*, 1986). This involves a systematic procedure in which teachers look at some aspect of their own or the school's practice which is giving rise to some concern, identify the precise nature of the problem, collect some data concerning the problem, and then devise, implement and evaluate a solution. Many teachers have used this approach to develop some aspect of their teaching skills, ranging from dealing with new approaches to teaching and learning (such as the use of more small-group work) to simply improving skills that are already well-developed (such as the quality of giving individual help). Studies reporting the efforts of experienced teachers to develop their teaching skills well-illustrate that all teachers, not just beginning teachers, are continually involved in such development. Indeed, it is the sense that teaching skills continually need development to improve one's own practice and to meet new demands that makes teaching such a challenging profession.

Stages of development

Perrott (1982), in her analysis of how teaching skills are acquired and developed, focuses on three stages. The first stage is cognitive and involves developing an awareness, by study and observation, of what the skill is, identifying the various elements of the skill and their sequencing, knowing the purpose of using the skill, and knowing how it will benefit your teaching. The second stage she identifies as practice, normally in the classroom, but occasionally in a controlled setting as part of a training course in which there is a short practice of a specific skill. The third stage is feedback which enables the teacher to improve the performance of the skill by evaluating the relative success of its performance. Such feedback can range from simply an impressionistic sense of its successful performance to detailed feedback given by an observer, the use of audio-visual recording, or systematic data collected from pupils concerning their work, behaviour or opinions. Perrott sees this three-stage process as a cycle, in which the third stage feeds back into the first stage as part of an on-going development of the skill.

Having the ability to develop your skills

While it is clear that teachers are continually reflecting upon and practising their skills, it is also evident that this does not automatically lead to skilled performance. There are many teachers who, after years of experience, still have evident shortcomings in some teaching skills. In part, this reflects the fact that skilled performance also depends on ability and motivation. The teacher needs the ability to profit from reflection and practice, and the motivation to do so. If we consider questioning skills as an example, clearly all teachers need to develop such skills. However, while some teachers have built up great skills in the variety and range of question types they use and the skill with which they target pupils and elicit and elaborate pupils' responses, other experienced teachers may still show shortcomings in these respects. Why should this be so?

Earlier, I argued that skills involve knowledge, decision-making and action. All three of these elements are subject to the various general abilities of teachers. The teacher may simply not have built up the knowledge about the effective use of questioning skills, or have difficulties in making the appropriate decisions which use that knowledge, or have difficulties in carrying out the actions required in a skilled manner.

If we extend the example of questioning skills further, an example where the fault lies with inadequate knowledge would be a teacher who was simply unaware of the educational importance and benefits of using 'open' questions (questions where a number of correct answers are possible) as well as 'closed' questions (questions where only one correct answer is acceptable). An example where the fault lies with decision-making would be an inappropriate decision to simply repeat the same question to a pupil having a difficulty answering, rather than to phrase the question in a different way or perhaps provide a hint. An example where the fault lies in action would be a teacher who is unable to ask a question in a clear and unambiguous way. The relevant general abilities of the teacher involved here may not simply be intellectual ones, since much skilled performance depends on aspects of the teacher's personality or even acting ability. Some teachers find it easier than others to continually ask questions sounding as though they are genuinely curious and interested in the replies, or to tolerate the longer pauses of silence required to give pupils time to think when being asked a more complex question.

Practise your exposition

Being motivated to develop your skills

Developing teaching skills also depends on the teacher's motivation. Teachers vary immensely in the extent to which they are prepared to invest time, energy and effort to reflect upon, evaluate and improve their teaching skills. This is particularly a problem once a teacher has developed a sufficiently adequate range of teaching skills to give satisfactory lessons. Teaching often then becomes a matter of routine. This can become even more confirmed once various materials, examples and strategies have been prepared and practised.

In addition, to some extent, teachers' approaches to lessons tend to play to their own strengths. Thus, for example, a teacher who finds lessons generally work well if based on worksheets, close monitoring of progress, and one-to-one help, but in contrast finds lessons involving group work and class discussion tend to become noisy and chaotic, is more likely to design lessons based on the former than to develop and extend the skills involved in making the latter type of lessons successful. Indeed, one of the main reasons underlying the hostility against a particular curriculum innovation that may be felt by some teachers relates to the changes in their general approach and teaching skills required by the innovation. It says much for the professional commitment and sense of vocation of teachers, that the vast majority do spend much time and effort in continuing to develop their teaching skills and to develop new approaches to their teaching in the educational interests of their pupils.

Your professional development

It is also important to note that the responsibility to develop and extend your teaching skills is not simply your personal responsibility. Rather, it is also in part the responsibility of those within the school and agencies outside the school to ensure that such development is facilitated as part of your professional development, and as part of staff development at the school as a whole.

Mention has already been made of teacher appraisal and of the impetus that comes from curriculum innovation. Equally important, however, is the climate that exists within the school to facilitate the development of teaching skills as an on-going process. Waterhouse (1983), for example, argues that some characteristics of a positive climate for developing teaching skills include:

- a sense of common ownership amongst staff for the educational aims to be achieved
- a constant generation of ideas
- sharing problems
- mutual support

- respect for each other's opinions
- an open and co-operative approach to dealing with conflicts and crises
- allowing styles to vary according to situations and needs
- encouraging anyone, not just leaders, to propose improvements
- an 'organic' rather than 'bureaucratic' management style (the former being more informal and flexible, with decision-making shared rather than directed from the top through a hierarchy, and with less emphasis on reports and record keeping).

Finally, it is worth bearing in mind that, despite the immense importance of developing sound teaching skills and seeing this as an on-going process throughout your teaching career, teaching also involves a whole host of other important demands, both inside and outside the classroom. The reality of life as a teacher requires a prioritising and monitoring of the whole range of skills in doing your job effectively, and it will be both normal and sensible to find that skills other than those considered here will occasionally need attention. Perhaps it is best to view the development of your teaching skills as a process which is always in operation, but which varies in intensity depending on the situation and context you find yourself in. If your teaching is to retain the sharpness, freshness and cutting edge that characterises the most effective teaching, it is crucial that your skills are never allowed to rest for too long on the back burner.

2 Planning and preparation

The key task facing teachers is to set up a learning activity which effectively achieves the learning outcomes intended for each pupil. At the start of a lesson, all teachers need to have some idea of what learning they wish to take place and how the lesson will facilitate that learning. While student teachers on teaching practice are usually required to make explicit lesson plans, experienced teachers more often rely on their extensive experience to form a mental framework of how they want the lesson to proceed. This does not necessarily mean that the lesson plans of established teachers are any less detailed than those of beginning teachers, simply that the lesson plans have become internalised through repetition.

The elements of planning and preparation

There are four major elements involved in the planning and preparation of a lesson:

1 *A decision about the educational objectives* that the lesson will be designed to foster.
2 *A selection and scripting of a lesson,* which involves deciding on the type and nature of activities to be used (eg exposition, group work, reading), the order and timing of each of these activities, and the content and materials to be used.
3 *A preparation of all the props* to be used, including materials, worked examples, checking that apparatus is ordered, delivered and in working order, arranging the layout of the classroom, and, in occasional circumstances, even a rehearsal (such as when a new experiment or demonstration is involved).
4 *A decision regarding how you will monitor and assess pupils' progress* and attainment during and after the lesson to evaluate whether the intended learning has taken place.

Meeting the needs of learners
The HMI (1988b), in their evaluation of lessons, focused on two crucial aspects in relation to planning and preparation. First, is it clear what the purpose of the lesson is? Second, has the lesson taken adequate account of the learners' needs? The former question addresses the question of how clearly specified the educational objectives of the lesson

were. The latter question addresses the extent to which the educational objectives take adequate account of the range and type of pupils' abilities, their previous learning, and their progress towards future educational attainment.

It is perhaps the teacher's sensitivity to pupils' needs that is the most important of all the skills involved in effective teaching. This refers to the ability of the teacher to plan lessons and adapt and modify their delivery by taking account of how the lesson will be experienced by different pupils and foster their learning. It is impossible and meaningless to attempt to evaluate the quality of a lesson plan without taking into account how well it meets the needs of the pupils in the context in which it will take place.

Educational objectives

Selecting the educational objectives for a lesson is no mean task. At the very least, they must contribute to broad educationally worthwhile aims. However, fashions change, and what is regarded as worthwhile at one time (eg rote memorisation of the ports around the British coastline) may now be considered inappropriate. Many schools list a number of educational aims in their prospectuses. The aims of the National Curriculum, as specified in the 1988 Education Reform Act, lay down an important framework. This states that the school's curriculum should:

- promote the spiritual, moral, cultural, mental and physical development of pupils at the school and of society
- prepare such pupils for the opportunities, responsibilities and experiences of adult life.

The delivery of the aims of the National Curriculum is specified in great detail in terms of particular Attainment Targets to be fostered during pupils' school careers. Nevertheless, even the great detail of the National Curriculum can only provide a broad framework for the planning of individual lessons.

In selecting educational objectives, the teacher is obliged to specify clear learning outcomes which can usefully be analysed in terms of knowledge, understanding, skills and attitudes. This planning is extremely complex because a teacher inevitably has a range of outcomes in mind for a particular lesson, and indeed, the outcomes intended may differ markedly between the pupils in the class. In addition, all lessons involve an interplay between intellectual development (defined primarily in terms of a growth in pupils' knowledge, understanding and skills) and social development (defined primarily in terms of a growth in pupils' self-esteem and self-confidence in themselves as learners, an increased positive attitude towards the subject, and a greater maturity in their behaviour and interactions with others in the class). A teacher may thus have the development of an understanding of the concept of area as a major educational objective for a particular lesson. At the same time, there may be an overlay of other objectives in operation, such as the intention to give a particular able pupil the opportunity to do some extended work on this topic, the intention to help and encourage a pupil who has been showing a recent lack of interest, and the intention to use this topic to show that doing mathematics is fun and relates to important real-life applications. Only by being aware of such differing intentions can an observer make sense of the teacher's behaviour in the lesson.

Teachers' use of objectives in planning

While the notion of setting educational objectives is widely agreed to be an essential aspect of planning, Calderhead (1984) has argued that research on teachers' planning indicates that teachers do not start their planning by identifying educational objectives and then designing a lesson to deliver these objectives. Rather, it is more a problem-solving process, addressing the problem of how to structure the time and experience of pupils.

I think the problem of interpretation here lies in the fact that if you ask a teacher to talk about their planning of a lesson, the educational objectives for the lesson are often left implicit and greater attention is devoted to the activities to be employed. Indeed, Clark and Yinger (1987) have argued that there is clear research evidence that teachers do think about educational objectives in planning their lessons, but that this is often made more explicit by teachers when they talk about the thinking that occurs during and after a lesson. Overall, it appears that part of the problem in identifying how and when teachers specify the educational objectives for a lesson concerns how they articulate their thoughts to others.

The purposes and functions of planning

There are a number of important purposes and functions to the planning of lessons which are worth noting. First and foremost, it enables you to think clearly and specifically about the type of learning you wish to occur in a particular lesson, and to relate the educational objectives to what you know about the pupils and the place of the lesson in the general programme of study.

Second, it enables you to think about the structure and content of the lesson. This includes, most importantly, thinking about how long to devote to each activity. Indeed, one of the most important skills in teaching is that of judging how much time should be spent on each activity in a lesson and the best pace of progress through the activities.

Third, planning quite considerably reduces how much thinking you will have to do during the lesson. Once the lesson is in progress, there will be much to think about in order to maintain its effectiveness. The fact that the lesson as a whole has been well-planned means that you can normally focus your attention on the fine-tuning of the lesson, rather than trying to make critical decisions on the hop. Indeed, many decisions about a lesson can only adequately be taken in advance. For example, if it becomes evident that a map is needed during a lesson, there may be little you can do about it if you had not realised this during your planning and had one available. A related point to this is that being under pressure is not a good state to be in when trying to make sensible decisions about teaching. You can all too easily find that trying to direct or alter the course of a lesson while teaching can lead to difficulties until you have developed with experience a good sense of what will work and how, in the circumstances you face.

Fourth, planning leads on to the preparation of all the materials, resources and props in general that will be needed. For example, having some work ready prepared for any pupils who might finish the intended work for the lesson well ahead of the majority, or a summary of some key points you wish to recap between two activities, all enable the lesson to progress more smoothly and effectively.

A fifth important purpose of planning is that keeping your notes will provide a useful record for your future planning, particularly in relation to giving a similar lesson to another group of pupils and in your planning of future work with the pupils which will extend what they have done in that particular lesson. Indeed, it is very useful, particularly in the early years of teaching, to make a brief note at the end of each lesson of any points you want to draw to your attention at some future time when you need to refer to the lesson notes again.

Time spent planning

The amount of time spent planning also varies immensely between teachers and for the same teacher between lessons. While beginning teachers will certainly need to spend more time planning, some of the differences between teachers at the same level of experience seem to relate to their general style or approach to planning. In essence, some teachers feel more secure and relaxed about the tasks of teaching if a lesson has been well-planned. Others, to some extent, need the pressure generated by the close onset of a lesson to concentrate their minds to the task at hand. Certainly, the ideal approach will be one in which the teacher is able to devote some time, well in advance, to the planning of each lesson. The reality of life as a teacher, however, is that there are many competing demands on your time. The amount of time for planning is thus severely constrained. As a result, more extensive and formal planning is likely to occur only for those lessons where something new or more demanding will take place.

Be flexible in your lesson planning

Flexibility

Another very important aspect of planning is the need to be flexible about the implementation of your plans. Effective teaching depends on the ability to monitor, adapt and develop what goes on in the classroom in the light of how pupils behave during the lesson. No matter how careful and well thought out the planning of the lesson was, once it starts, the immediate demands of how things are going take complete precedence.

It may become apparent that some of the ideas you intended to introduce and discuss at length appear to be well-understood by pupils already or are much more difficult to understand than you envisaged; or you may notice that a large number of pupils are having difficulties in carrying out a task you had set and had planned to allow them to undertake largely uninterrupted for most of the lesson. In such circumstances, a change in your original plan would be appropriate to ensure that the pupils' needs were being met.

Unfortunately, beginning teachers are occasionally in the position of reaping the worst of both worlds. They invest a great deal of time and energy in preparing their plan for a lesson and at the same time have a greater need to be flexible and adapt their plan in the light of on-going feedback. Thus, for example, a worksheet may have been carefully prepared only to find the tasks set are too difficult, and a swift change to whole class teaching may be required. For experienced teachers such a circumstance is less likely to occur, but if it did, changing to another activity would pose little problem. For the beginning teacher, the circumstance is more likely, and the difficulty of switching to an unprepared activity more demanding. Indeed, because of this, student teachers are particularly likely to persist with their original plan unless the problems arising are much more acute and, until they build up experience, are more often than not wise to do so. In contrast, changing horses in mid-stream, to switch from one activity to a more appropriate one, is almost a skill of delight for the experienced teacher, in the extent to which it calls upon their professional knowledge and experience to be able to do so successfully.

Lesson planning

As noted earlier, there are four major elements involved in lesson planning:

- deciding on educational objectives
- selecting and scripting a lesson
- preparing the props to be used
- deciding how to monitor and assess pupils' progress.

The preparation of props will be considered in the final section of this chapter. The other three elements will be the focus of our attention in this section.

Deciding on educational objectives

The most important aspect of an educational objective is that it is a description of an aspect of pupil learning. To gain knowledge about prime numbers, to understand the nature of causality in history, to acquire the skill of drawing a river's path through contour lines, or to feel empathy for the victims of the slave trade, would all be examples of educational objectives for a lesson contributing to pupils' intellectual development.

To develop skills involved in co-operating with other pupils, to listen attentively to other pupils' statements during class discussion, and to feel more confident about one's own capabilities in the subject, would be examples of educational objectives for a lesson contributing to pupils' social development.

Educational objectives cannot be stated in terms of what pupils will be doing, such as working through an exercise, drawing a map or small-group discussion. These are activities used to promote learning. The educational objectives must describe what is to constitute the learning. One of the major pitfalls in teaching is to neglect thinking precisely about educational objectives and to see planning as simply organising activities. While the two go hand-in-hand, it is all too easy to think that a lesson that went well logistically (*viz* pupils did what you intended) was effective, until you ask yourself what the pupils actually learned.

In selecting your objectives, a great deal of thought needs to be given to how these objectives relate to previous and future work the pupils are involved in, and how appropriate they are to extending their current abilities, attitudes and interests. For example, in deciding to introduce the notion of prime numbers, do the pupils already have an adequate grasp of what it means for numbers to have factors? Indeed, linking new learning to previous learning is immensely important, and particularly effective if the new learning can be seen to grow out of the previous learning. Thus, a lesson on prime numbers may first of all utilise an activity in which pupils can apply their previous knowledge and understanding of factors (this will check that all is well on that front). They may then identify numbers only divisible by one and itself, which are then given a special name (prime numbers). This would combine a linking of previous learning with a sense of discovery and growth, and also extend that previous learning.

Selecting content

Selecting the content for a lesson involves a number of considerations. Even working within the framework of the National Curriculum still leaves a great deal of choice to teachers. The selection of content will clearly need to relate to the overall programme of study for pupils, but the decision concerning how much emphasis to give to particular topics will depend on the teacher's view of its importance and difficulty.

Indeed, a very important teaching skill is that of separating a topic into distinct elements or aspects, and designing a sequence or progression through these elements that makes coherent and intellectual sense and effectively facilitates learning. One of the most demanding aspects of beginning teaching is trying to decide how best to do this in a way that satisfactorily meets the pupils' needs. This demands good subject knowledge by the teacher, an awareness of how to separate and sequence the elements of the topic, and an awareness of pupils' needs. Beginning teachers tend to rely somewhat on established practice in the school, particularly if a scheme of work is in use (such as that based on a textbook or worksheets). With experience, however, teachers become much more confident and authoritative in deciding on the nature and structure of the content they wish to use, and also better able to judge the pace of progress to expect through the content elements and the likely areas of difficulty or misunderstanding that may arise. The problem for experienced teachers becomes that of keeping abreast of developments in the teaching of their subject and topics in line with changes in required educational attainment.

Selecting learning activities

The selection of learning activities offers much scope and choice for teachers. The decision about which activity or combination of activities to use within a lesson depends on the teacher's beliefs about the relative effectiveness of the different activities for the type of pupil learning intended. This decision, however, also needs to take account of a range of factors concerning the context of the lesson.

First, will the activities selected meet the needs of this particular group of pupils, taking account of their abilities, interests and motivation, and the way they are likely to respond to these activities? You may feel that because a particular class seems to work well when group work tasks are used, that you will incorporate group work into their lesson. Equally well, you may decide to incorporate group work into the lesson because the class has not worked well with this activity, and you feel more practice and experience of this activity will be of value to them in developing associated skills and benefits. Indeed, the fact that an activity has not worked well may suggest a need to use it more often rather than to avoid using it at all.

A second important factor concerns when the lesson occurs. The type of activities that might be effective on a Friday afternoon or following morning assembly, or extending work done in a previous lesson when a number of learning difficulties were encountered, may well be influenced by this context.

Third, such planning decisions are also influenced by logistics, other demands and time pressures facing the teacher. A lesson which requires a lot of planning effort and preparation is perhaps best avoided in the middle of a week in which you have to mark a heavy load of examination scripts, or when particular equipment needed is in great demand for other activities.

The variety and appropriateness of activities

When thinking about the learning activities to be used, you also need to think of the lesson as a coherent whole, such that the total package of experience provided for pupils achieves your intended learning outcomes. As such, not only must the activities deliver the appropriate intellectual experience for this learning to occur, but also facilitate the ease with which pupils can engage and remain engaged in this experience.

The activities must thus elicit and sustain pupils' attention, interest and motivation. Even when interest and motivation are high, pupils will find it difficult to listen to a teacher's exposition for a long period, doubly so if they are young or the exposition is difficult or unclear, or if it is a hot day. As such, most lessons will involve some variety of activities. The initial phase of the lesson may be designed to set the scene and elicit interest, the major part of the lesson may involve the main learning experiences, and the ending may involve some recap or general comments about the importance, relevance or quality of the learning that took place.

While a variety of activities is important, each activity must be appropriate to the learning at hand. Thus, for example, developing pupils' ability to articulate and communicate their ideas orally is much more likely to be achieved through practise, feedback and critiquing others, rather than in extensive reading or listening to theory about how to do it (although the latter may play a useful part). A variety of activities also provides pupils with an opportunity to learn in different ways, and thereby to build up and develop the skills to do so effectively. At the same time, however, this does not mean that every lesson must involve a variety of activities. It is just as important to provide extended periods of work based on one type of task in order to allow pupils to develop the skills of organising and sustaining their concentration and effort, particularly in relation to a task where the quality of what is produced depends on the marshalling and development of the work undertaken (in contrast to a simply repetitive task).

Monitoring and assessing pupils' progress

Once the lesson has begun, you will need to monitor and assess pupils' progress and attainment to ensure that the lesson is being effective and is likely to deliver the pupil learning intended. At the same time, this will also give you feedback on what aspects of the lesson, as originally planned, need on-going modification and adaptation to maintain effectiveness. This requires more than just being responsive and reactive to feedback, such as waiting for a pupil to say they do not understand how to approach the task set. Rather, it requires you to be active, and to probe, question, check and test whether the progress and attainment intended is occurring.

While there is much feedback available to the teacher simply by looking at pupils' facial expressions or responding to those who confess to having difficulties, all too often most pupils will adopt strategies and techniques which indicate superficially that they understand and can do the work set. Only when exercise books are collected in, or questions asked at the end of a lesson, or subsequent tests given, might it become evident that much less learning was going on than appeared to be the case.

You should regularly assess your pupils' progress

Unfortunately, it is all too easy to avoid active probing of progress and attainment; if the lesson appears to be going well, you naturally feel that to do so will be making problems for yourself that will need to be dealt with. It requires a great deal of integrity on the teacher's part to, in essence, look for trouble. However, that is in fact the very cutting edge of the skill involved here. Simply approaching a pupil who appears to be working well and asking 'How are things going?' and probing with a few telling questions, can often reveal difficulties that either the pupil was not aware of, or was even deliberately trying to avoid your noticing. Indeed, Pye (1988) has graphically described just how well some pupils manage to avoid being noticed by teachers, by avoiding eye contact and appearing to be working well whenever the teacher was nearby.

Such active monitoring and assessment of pupils requires some forethought and planning. At what stages during the lesson and how are you going to get the necessary feedback? For example, one may usefully use a transition period between one activity and another for some quick whole-class questioning and discussion about what was covered and whether any problems have arisen. This does not mean that every lesson must have some in-built testing of attainment; rather, a more subtle form of on-going probing and recapping should be employed which will be sufficient to enable the teacher to feel confident that the intended learning is occurring. Nevertheless, there is a role here for formal tests from time to time, and occasionally the use of homework to explicitly probe the learning covered rather than to generate new learning.

Prop preparation

Preparation primarily refers to the preparation of all the props to be used in the lesson, including the writing and running off of copies of worksheets, the ordering, delivery and checking of equipment, arranging desks and chairs in the required layout, and making notes about the content of the lesson to be presented. Clearly, planning and preparation go hand-in-hand and many planning decisions are taken while preparation is going on. Nevertheless, there are a number of important skills involved in preparation that are worthy of attention and may be crucial to the effectiveness of the lesson.

Showing you care

The care and effort that teachers take over preparation can have a major positive impact on pupils' sense that the teacher cares about their learning and that the activities to be undertaken are worthwhile and important. In contrast, a lack of preparation, such as may be evident if the teacher has to leave the room at a crucial point to find some statistical tables that need to be handed out, does not simply disrupt the flow of the lesson, but may be perceived by pupils as insulting to their sense of worth as learners (if our learning were really important, the teacher would have prepared better).

While such problems will occur from time to time even in the best-prepared circumstances, and pupils will tolerate these, the regular occurrence of poor preparation must be avoided. To be able to say in the middle of a lesson, 'I have already prepared for you ...', and then reveal some materials, equipment, or even pull down a rotating blackboard to reveal a diagram or set of key questions, can have a marked rousing effect on pupils' self-esteem, enthusiasm and sense of purpose for the next part of the lesson.

Rehearsal, checking and back-up

The use of any sort of equipment always poses potential problems for the teacher. Three key words are relevant here: rehearsal, checking and back-up. If you are going to use equipment or materials for any sort of experiment or practical work, you will often find it useful and worthwhile to have a rehearsal of some sort before you deliver that lesson for the first time. Practicals that appear to be virtually problem-proof can have surprises in store for you. For example, you may find that the length of time it takes for a particular effect to be visible takes much longer than you planned for.

Another problem can arise if the equipment available is different in some way from that you have used in the past. Some lessons will also require testing the equipment for its purpose. For example, if you are going to take a group of pupils pond-dipping, you may want to check on the type of creatures currently in the pond and whether the jars, nets or whatever is needed are available. Another aspect of rehearsal involves trying to experience the use of the equipment and materials from the pupils' perspective. In preparing an overhead transparency, for example, is what is projected onto the screen clear and readable from the back of the classroom? In using some authentic audio-tapes of French conversation, is the sound clear at the back of the room? In making a construction from card, is the card too flimsy or too hard for its purpose?

Checking simply refers to the need to ensure shortly before the lesson is due to start, that all the props needed are to hand and in good working order. For anything electrical, this is almost mandatory. Such checking is made easier if you have starred on your lesson notes those items that need a check in this way. Nevertheless, even with adequate rehearsal and checking, things will happen that require a change in your lesson plan. It is here that some thought to back-up can be extremely helpful. While you cannot have a back-up for every piece of equipment, as a matter of regular practice it is always worth having a spare lightbulb attached to an overhead projector. More appropriately, you do need to think of what you will do if a particular piece of equipment fails, or the lesson grinds to a halt for some other reason. In planning a lesson, some thought, even if only limited, can be usefully devoted to how another part of the lesson or some alternative activity can be used to good effect if problems arise.

Teaching materials

Worksheets, overhead transparencies, task cards and computer software packages are commonly employed, and their design and use involve a number of preparation skills. Often it is important to regard such preparation as a team activity, shared with colleagues, rather than something you do in isolation. Resources of this sort can be used many times over and as such, if they can be designed to fit well into the programmes of study, used by colleagues, and can be linked carefully to assessment tests, then the time spent in producing high-quality items will be well worthwhile.

However, before embarking on such preparation, it is a good idea to explore whether such resources are already available and can be purchased, borrowed or copied. Some textbook schemes provide a set of parallel worksheets that can be used. Local teachers' centres often contain a whole host of well-prepared resources of a high quality that can be adapted and used for your purposes. Some schools have gone to great lengths to develop and catalogue materials into a resources centre, either school-wide based or subject-specific. Brown (1987), for example, has shown how many infant school teachers were well-organised in this respect in how they formed a collection of pictures that could be used for a whole variety of learning purposes to good effect. There are many excellent resources and activity packs now published, including mathematical games, facsimile documents for historical analysis, and computer simulations for scientific processes, all of a quality well beyond that which teachers can normally produce. Nevertheless, one always needs to ensure that any materials used are appropriate to the learning outcomes intended, and not used simply because they are readily available. Indeed, the HMI (1988b) have been critical of an over-reliance on commercial schemes that have not been adequately considered in terms of their contribution to the educational objectives intended for the programme of study.

In preparing worksheets, task cards or similar types of materials, quality of presentation is of the highest importance. They need to be well laid out, not contain too much information, and should attempt to elicit pupils' interest. Particular attention needs to be paid to the language used; you need to be sure it is neither too simple nor too difficult for the range of pupil ability for whom it is intended. You also need to give careful thought as to whether such materials are going to be introduced by you and supplemented with various instructions, or whether they are to be self-explanatory. Worksheets and task cards can range from simple exercises and tasks aimed at extracting facts from what is given to answer the questions posed, to quite sophisticated materials aimed to give pupils an opportunity for creative analysis.

An example of the former is a worksheet on percentages containing cut-out adverts from a newspaper concerning the prices of various items with percentage reductions; questions here may involve calculating which items were the best buys. An example of the latter is a series of line-drawn pictures (as in children's comics) about which pupils have to write a story. As well as examples designed to be used by individual pupils, other materials can be designed for small-group work, such as using a facsimile of a letter written by a king as a source of evidence to interpret a historial event (also taking account of when and to whom the letter was written as part of the discussion of the letter as valid evidence); here the use of small-group discussion may highlight the extent to which interpretation and validity of evidence involve personal judgements.

Assessment materials

Preparation skills also include the need to prepare assessment materials. Indeed, the monitoring of pupils' progress and attainment throughout their school careers requires a formal and regular record to be kept.

While some of this will involve formal tests given at the end of periods of study, much assessment is also based on observing performance during normal classroom activity.

This is particularly so in relation to monitoring the development of various pupil skills and competencies defined in the National Curriculum. This requires that appropriate assessments are prepared and built into the planning of lessons, and a formal note made of pupils' performance. This means that some activities in the lesson will be deliberately planned with a view to an assessment being made. As such, the activity must offer a fair opportunity to monitor the performance being examined. Two important planning decisions are involved here. First, how many pupils will you attempt to assess in a particular lesson (one, several, all)? Second, what procedures will you adopt (will you tell pupils that a formal assessment is being made?; will you help pupils having difficulties during the assessment, and, if so, how will you take this into account in your recording?)?

In designing assessment materials to be used during normal classroom activity, particular care needs to be taken to ensure that they validly explore the learning you intend to examine. This involves not only assessing what it purports to assess, but assessing it in the way and to the degree required. Consider, for example, such skills as these involved in National Curriculum Science:

- to be able to use simple power sources and devices which transfer energy
- to be able to measure forces
- to be able to argue, with the aid of supporting evidence, that the Earth is not flat.

Before being able to even begin to prepare the assessment materials and procedures, the teacher will need to be clear about the nature and precision required for the assessment. In addition, for such assessments to be fair, the materials and procedures adopted will need to be standardised so that each pupil is assessed in the same way.

Record keeping
Advanced thought and planning about how records are to be made and kept is also required. These will almost certainly need to be developed and agreed with other colleagues, so that the school's records will be consistent and coherent as the pupils progress through their school careers. A variety of assessment materials need to be used and types of responses given (based on direct observations of pupils' behaviour, questioning in verbal and written form, paper and pencil tests, and derived from normal coursework, including homework).

Preparing yourself and pupils

Another aspect of preparation is the need to prepare yourself. While most teachers can teach most topics most of the time with little need to stimulate their subject knowledge, there will be some topics where you will need to learn about the topic in advance of teaching about it. In that sense, you will literally only be one jump ahead of the pupils. Indeed, in areas of rapid curriculum development, you will be hard pressed even to be ahead of the pupils! This means that private study of particular topics will be needed, ranging from making use of appropriate teacher guides that are available, to attending formal courses or workshop activities for teachers. At its best, the need to do this can add a sense of freshness and curiosity for these topics that you can share and delight in with your pupils.

In addition, you need to consider whether pupils need to be prepared in any way. You may need to give them advance warning of particular topics, particularly if they will need to do some preparatory reading, revise some previous work, or bring certain equipment or articles with them. In such circumstances, you also need to check that they are prepared as required, and you may need to have spares of the equipment available. Indeed, in some schools, having spare pens to hand is almost essential for the smooth running of lessons.

Key questions about your planning and preparation

1 *Are my educational objectives for this lesson clear?*

2 *Do my educational objectives take appropriate account of pupils' needs, particularly in terms of their abilities, interests, motivation, the context of the lesson, and the work they have previously done and will do in the future as part of their programme of study?*

3 *Does the content matter of the lesson and the learning activities selected, together with the structure of the lesson, appear appropriate to maintain pupils' interest and motivation, and deliver the educational objectives intended?*

4 *What type of pupil performance during the lesson can I expect, and how do I monitor and explore pupils' progress to ensure that the lesson is effectively promoting the intended pupil learning?*

5 *Are all the materials, resources and equipment I require well-prepared and checked?*

6 *Does my lesson plan contain all the notes I need to refer to, including, for example, worked examples or a note about extension work to be used if the need arises?*

7 *Have I adequately prepared pupils for this lesson, by alerting them in advance to any revision that may be required or other preparation they should do beforehand?*

8 *Am I prepared for this lesson, in terms of my subject matter knowledge about the topic to be covered?*

9 *What type of assessment will I be conducting during the lesson, and, if formal assessment is occurring, is this well-planned and prepared?*

10 *Are there any particular concerns that I need to bear in mind regarding this lesson, such as a pupil with special educational needs, or a particular aspect of the topic or learning activity that will require careful monitoring?*

3 Lesson presentation

Lesson presentation refers to the learning experiences you set up to achieve the intended learning outcomes by pupils. As a result of the many different types of teaching methods that have been developed, there is now a staggering range of learning activities available that can be deployed to good effect, including, by way of example, exposition, practicals, worksheets, computer games, role play and small-group discussion. Moreover, teachers are actively encouraged and expected to make use of a variety of teaching methods in their programme of lessons.

In considering learning activities that a teacher can use, a useful distinction can be made between those activities largely dependent on teacher talk and those that can proceed with little or no direct teacher participation. The former will include teacher exposition, teacher questioning, and, to a greater or lesser extent, classroom discussion channelled through the teacher. I shall call these *teacher talk activities*. The latter will include, for example, practicals, investigational and problem-solving activities, worksheets, computer games, role play and small-group discussion. I shall call these *academic tasks*. These two classes of activities will be discussed later in this chapter. Before doing so, however, it is important to consider first of all another aspect of lesson presentation: the teacher's manner.

The teacher's manner

When it comes to lesson presentation, the way that you do it is just as important as what you do. Asking a question with interest conveyed in your tone of voice and facial expression, as opposed to sounding tired and bored, makes a world of difference to the type of response you will get, no matter how appropriate the actual question was. Similarly, circulating around the room to monitor progress and help anyone who is in difficulties, rather than sitting at your desk at the front marking work from another lesson, also conveys an attitude to pupils about the importance of the lesson. All such cues together create a general impression regarding how much effort you feel it is worthwhile to put into the lesson to ensure pupil learning takes place. To elicit and sustain effective learning by pupils, in general, your manner needs to be confident, relaxed, self-assured, purposeful and should generate an interest in the lesson. In addition, you need to exude positive expectations concerning the progress you expect to occur during the lesson.

Positive cues about your manner
There are a number of skills involved in conveying to pupils that you are confident, relaxed, self-assured and purposeful. However, the most crucial aspect to doing this is that you *are* in fact confident, relaxed, self-assured and purposeful! The starting point is not one of being nervous and anxious, and then thinking how you can convey that you are relaxed and confident. Rather, the starting point should be that by sound planning and preparation, and with developing experience, you will quite naturally and unconsciously convey these positive cues. Nevertheless, there are times, particulary when beginning a career in teaching, or occasionally when things are going wrong, that you will feel anxious. In such circumstances it is helpful to try to consciously induce a sense of relaxation as far as possible, and also to be aware of the aspect of your behaviour involved in conveying this.

The positive cues are largely conveyed by your facial expression, tone of voice, speech, use of eye contact, gestures and positioning. When you feel nervous, you will naturally tend to look and sound nervous, avoid eye contact, and make awkward or repetitive gestures. As such, when feeling nervous, consciously make an effort to ensure that your speech is fluid, clear and audible, that you maintain regular eye contact with pupils and scan around the classroom, and that you spend time standing centre-stage at the front and erect when appropriate.

For the vast majority of beginning teachers, such skills develop fairly quickly; for others, it takes somewhat longer. Some student teachers appear to feel at home in the classroom from the very first lesson; others only start to feel really relaxed and confident during their first year or two of teaching. It must be recognised, however, that there are some for whom the act of teaching will always be anxiety provoking. For those who are unable to feel at home in the classroom, most will not pursue a career in teaching for long. This largely reflects the fact that although much of the teacher's manner can develop through training and experience, it is in part bound up with the person's personality. This is why it is so important for beginning teachers to capitalise on their own strengths and mitigate their shortcomings, rather than attempt to model themselves on any particular style of teaching they have witnessed or is being advocated to them.

Other important aspects of your manner
Over the years there has been much discussion and research concerning other aspects of the teacher's manner which contribute to effective teaching, and it must be said that no clear and consistent picture has

emerged. Undoubtedly, this is because it is possible to be effective through different means. For one teacher, the key to success may largely stem from being firm; for another, it may stem from a warm and caring attitude. Nevertheless, in general, it does appear that the quality of conveying enthusiasm and interest for the subject matter at hand is important. Less consistently supported by research evidence, although widely advocated, are the qualities of patience and a sense of humour (eg see Good and Brophy (1987) for an overview). For example, in a survey of sixth-formers' attitudes concerning effective teaching, teacher enthusiasm and interest for the subject, patience and a sense of humour were generally associated with fostering greater educational attainment (Kyriacou, 1986b).

Teacher talk activities

Teachers spend a great deal of their time talking, whether it be lecturing, explaining, giving instructions, asking questions, or directing whole-class discussion. As such, it is not surprising that the quality of teacher talk is one of the most important aspects of effective teaching. Indeed, many would claim that it is the most important quality of effective teaching. In the study mentioned above (Kyriacou, 1986b), the sixth-formers rated the teacher's ability to explain points clearly and at the pupils' level as being associated with fostering greater educational attainment more highly than any other of the 38 teacher characteristics listed in the survey.

Exposition

There is a wealth of research evidence to support the claim that clarity of explanation (often referred to as 'teacher clarity') makes a major contribution to greater educational attainment. Teacher clarity certainly enhances teacher talk activities, and also makes a contribution to the extent that it is involved in academic tasks, such as may occur before, during or after a role-play activity, or in the content and layout of a worksheet (see Cruickshank and Kennedy (1986) for a review of such research evidence).

Teacher exposition (*viz* informing, describing and explaining) typically occurs at the start of a lesson, sometimes at the end, and also during a lesson, as and when the teacher feels it is appropriate. In schools, it rarely takes the form of a lecture for any great length of time, nor should it, as pupils will find it difficult to pay attention to a lecture, except for a short interval. Indeed, for this reason, many teachers use a series of questions and develop pupils' replies to trace out what they want to say, rather than lecture. This not only involves the pupils more, but also enables you to check on pupils' understanding.

Starting the lesson

The quality of teacher exposition at the start of the lesson can be particularly important as it serves a number of functions. First, it must elicit and sustain pupils' attention and interest in the lesson. Establishing a positive attitude at the start of the lesson provides a good springboard for what follows. To create a positive mental set, it is important to ensure that pupils are paying attention when the lesson begins.

Second, it is useful to indicate what the purpose or topic for the lesson is, and its importance or relevance. A question to the class, rather than a statement, can usefully arouse their curiosity and induce a problem-solving thrust towards what follows. A fairly quiet but audible voice level is best as it encourages listening, discourages background noise, and makes varying the tone and volume of your delivery easier. Having elicited attention, and indicated the purpose of the lesson, the third function of your introduction may usefully be to alert pupils to any links with previous lessons they need to be aware of, or any particular problems or aspects of this lesson they should be alert to, in order to best prepare them for what is to follow. Such preparation may even include practical matters concerning the equipment they will need to use or the pace at which they will be expected to work.

Effective explaining

Explaining often goes hand-in-hand with questioning, with the teacher switching from one to the other as and when appropriate. Often this switch is influenced by whether the teacher feels it is appropriate to pull ideas together swiftly to facilitate a move to the next phase of the lesson, using a synthesizing statement, or whether the teacher feels more involvement and probing of pupils' ideas is needed. For both explaining and questioning, it is particularly important to ensure that the nature and complexity of the language used by the teacher is at an appropriate level for pupils to understand. Indeed, the skill of the teacher to pitch language use appropriately by taking account of pupils' current level of understanding is one of the most important skills the beginning teacher needs to master.

Looking at the skills involved in effective explaining, Brown and Armstrong (1984) have identified five basic skills:

- *clarity and fluency*: through defining new terms clearly and appropriate use of explicit language
- *emphasis and interest*: making good use of voice, gestures, materials and paraphrasing
- *using examples*: appropriate in type and quality

- *organisation*: presence of a logical sequence and use of link words and phrases
- *feedback*: offering a chance for pupils to ask questions and assessing learning outcomes.

Perhaps the most important aspect of explaining, however, is the skill in deciding the size of step that pupils can take in going from what they knew at the start of the lesson to the learning you hope will have taken place by the end of the lesson. This decision about the size of step has crucial implications for the type and sophistication of the explanations offered.

In summary, explanations should by and large try to be grammatically simple, explicit, make good use of examples, define any technical terms and, most importantly, not go on for too long!

Questioning

Questioning skills are also central to the repertoire of effective teaching. There can be few professions to compare with teaching where you spend so much time every day asking questions to which you already know the answer. Brown and Edmondson (1984) have listed a number of reasons given by teachers for asking questions. In order of frequency, these were:

- to encourage thought, understanding of ideas, phenomena, procedures and values
- to check understanding, knowledge and skills
- to gain attention to task, to enable teacher to move towards teaching points, as a 'warm up' activity for pupils
- to review, revise, recall, reinforce a recently learned point, remind of earlier procedures
- to aid management, settling down, stop pupils calling out, direct attention to teacher or text, warn of precautions
- to teach the whole class through pupil answers
- to give everyone a chance to answer
- to use bright pupils to encourage others
- to draw in shyer pupils
- to probe pupils' knowledge after critical answers
- to allow expression of feelings, views and empathy.

Types of questions

A useful distinction can be made between 'open' and 'closed' questions. Open questions can have a number of right answers, whereas closed questions will only have one right answer. Another useful distinction can be made between 'higher-order' questions and 'lower-order' questions. Higher-order questions involve reasoning, analysis and evaluation, whereas lower-order questions are concerned with simple recall or comprehension.

Much research indicates that teachers overwhelmingly ask more closed and lower-order questions than open and higher-order questions, and this has often been cited as a cause for concern. While in general, open and higher-order questions are more intellectually demanding and stimulating, and research does indicate that more of these types of questions could usefully be asked, one does need to bear in mind the range of purposes behind asking questions, as indicated earlier. Given that open and higher-order questions are more time-consuming, it would be difficult to use these much more frequently without constraining other intentions, such as the need to maintain an appropriate pace to the lesson or to involve most of the pupils. As with all aspects of teaching skills, a balance is required in meeting a range of different intentions at the same time.

Effective questioning

Kerry (1982) has identified seven questioning skills:

- pitching the language and content level of questions appropriately for the class
- distributing questions around the class
- prompting and giving clues when necessary
- using pupils' responses (even incorrect ones) in a positive way
- timing questions and pauses between questions
- learning to make progressively greater cognitive demands through sequences of higher-order questions
- using written questions effectively.

When asking questions there are two extremely important points to bear in mind. First, answering a question, particularly in front of classmates, is an emotionally high-risk actively. As such, it is essential that the classroom climate during questioning is one of support and respect for the pupil's answer (both by the teacher and by other pupils). Second, do not allow some pupils to opt out of questioning. Pye (1988) has noted how some pupils are adept at avoiding being noticed and will do whatever they can to terminate quickly any interaction with the teacher. Such pupils need to be involved and helped to contribute to the lesson.

A number of features characterise skilful questioning. It is a useful technique not to name the pupil whom you want to answer the question until you have finished the question. This helps to ensure that all pupils are attentive. When asking the question, try to ensure that it is as clear and unambiguous as possible. If the pupil is in difficulties, it is always useful to rephrase the question in a different way. Most importantly, ask the question in a manner that conveys you are interested in the reply, maintain eye contact with the pupil and ensure that other pupils have the courtesy to listen in silence. When prompting or helping a pupil, remember that the object of this is to help the pupil's thinking, not to enable the correct answer to be guessed from the clues given. Finally, it is often worthwhile to check how a pupil arrived at the answer given (whether right or wrong), as this can give you some key insights into the thinking involved.

Directing classroom discussion

The third area of teacher talk activities to be considered here is that of classroom discussion channelled through the teacher: a mixture of teacher and pupil explanations, views and questions. Classroom discussion begins at the point when pupils ask questions and when one pupil responds to what another pupil has said.

When classroom discussion takes place, two key decisions you need to take concern: first, the layout of the room (is it appropriate to organise pupils so that they can see and hear each other?), and second,

Directing classroom discussion

the extent to which you are going to direct the discussion and make a leading contribution to shaping the flow and development of what is said. In using classroom discussion to good effect, it is useful to indicate the purpose of having such a discussion, to indicate how long the discussion is intended to last, and to summarise at the end what conclusions can be drawn. It is particularly important to remember that one of the prime reasons for having classroom discussion is to give pupils the opportunity to develop and express their ideas. This will need encouragement, and a tolerance to allow badly formed and incorrect notions to be expressed (ensuring that any errors become apparent as the discussion develops, rather than interrupted or shot down immediately).

Academic tasks

Academic tasks refer to activities set up by teachers to facilitate pupil learning, which can proceed with little or no direct teacher participation once they are up and running. Examples include practicals, investigational and problem-solving activities, worksheets, computer games, role play and small-group discussion. Almost all such activities tend to involve the teacher circulating around and monitoring progress, giving individual help as and when necessary. Nevertheless, some teachers prefer to maintain a high level of direction during such activities, while others see important educational benefits deriving from being less directive (this point will be developed further when we consider the notion of 'active learning' later in this chapter).

Setting up academic tasks

For academic tasks to be successfully employed, it is absolutely crucial that it is clear to pupils what they have to do, and to indicate the relationship between the task and the learning intended. It is easy to fall into the trap of thinking that the most important aspect is to get the pupils underway quickly with the task and then to deal with any problems as they arise. Doing so can lead to your having to dash from one desk to another throughout the lesson, or else having to interrupt the class as a whole on several occasions. In fact, the most important aspect for success is the careful preparation of the tasks and materials to be used (so that they are clear and, if necessary, self-explanatory) coupled with a clear briefing of what is required before the task is started. Some pupils may not pay attention during this briefing session if they know that you will simply give an individual briefing to anyone who wants one once the work has begun. If several pupils have this attitude, there will be many demands made on you at the start. As such, it is well worthwhile to ensure that as many pupils as possible are clear about the task in hand before the class is allowed to start the work.

Another aspect of academic tasks that is of great importance is to ensure that pupils possess the skills required to undertake the task successfully, or, if not, that the skills are helped to develop. All tasks, whether it be extracting information from a set text, using a worksheet, operating a computer package, carrying out a practical or participating in small-group discussion, involve a number of skills. It is all too easy to assume that pupils already have appropriate skills or can develop these by trial and error. In fact, a lot of pupils get into difficulties simply because they are unsure about how to proceed and what is expected of them.

A nice example of this problem is that of a teacher asking pupils to spend a lesson writing a poem about Winter. Now, for some pupils the processes involved in writing a poem are rather mysterious, and little headway may be made. However, if the teacher was first to spend a lesson composing a poem from scratch on the blackboard in front of the pupils, and demonstrating by thinking aloud how one can start from some ideas, phrases and re-work these and change words, the whole process for pupils can then be de-mystified. This de-mystification is essential for almost all academic tasks. How do you extract information from a set text? What is the point of small-group discussion? Paying explicit attention to pupils' learning skills before, during and after academic tasks can have a major impact on the quality of learning which takes place.

One of the advantages of setting work for individuals is that it allows pupils to work at their own pace, it helps them to organise and take responsibility for their own effort, and it enables the work to be structured and tailored to their own level of difficulty, providing extension and enrichment materials and tasks for the more able pupils in the class. Where pupils are working individually on an extended piece of work or project, or through a workscheme, careful and regular monitoring of progress is essential.

Co-operative activities

Co-operative activities, such as small-group discussion or collaborative problem solving, enable pupils to share ideas, to develop the skills involved in co-operative interaction, to communicate clearly and to work as a team. Generally speaking, a group size ranging from two to six seems to be best for most co-operative tasks.

The HMI (1987) have noted that some teachers are reluctant to make use of co-operative activities because they fear that by relinquishing tight control over the learning activities, it will be harder to sustain good order. There is little doubt that such activities do depend on good teaching skills, but fortunately with the increasing use of such activities, pupils are more familiar and more skilled at using such activities to good effect than when such activities were relatively novel in schools.

Active learning

Active learning refers to any activities where pupils are given a marked degree of autonomy and control over the organisation, conduct and direction of the learning activity. Most usually such activities involve problem-solving and investigational work, and may be individualised (such as an extended piece of work or project) or involve small-group collaboration (such as small-group discussion, a role-play simulation or a collaborative project).

In essence, active learning may usefully be contrasted with expository teaching, in which pupils are relatively passive receivers of information which is tightly under the teacher's control. A number of educational benefits have been claimed for active learning:

- such activities are intellectually more stimulating and thereby are more effective in eliciting and sustaining pupil motivation and interest in the activities
- such activities are effective in fostering a number of important learning skills involved in the process of organising the activities, such as when organising their own work during individualised activities, and interaction and communication skills during co-operative activities
- such activities are likely to be enjoyed, offer opportunity for progress, are less threatening than teacher talk activities and thereby foster more positive pupil attitudes towards themselves as learners and more positive attitudes towards the subject
- co-operative activities in particular enable greater insights to occur regarding the conduct of the learning activities through observing the performance of peers and sharing and discussing procedures and strategies.

In considering active learning, however, you need to be aware that this term has not been used by teachers with any consistency. As well as referring to teaching methods or learning activities, it is sometimes used to refer to the mental experience of learning by discovery (see Kyriacou and Marshall (1989) for an analysis). Nevertheless, in the sense of activities such as small-group work, teachers are generally expected to make use of such activities as well as teacher talk activities. The message, in effect, being that how pupils learn is as important as the content of what they learn.

In addition, active learning can sometimes offer a much more powerful experience or insight into what is to be learnt than expository teaching. For example, in a mathematics lesson, a teacher could ask pupils to guess how many pupils could fit into a one cubic metre box, and then bring one in and see. Pupils having this experience are thereafter left with a very strong image of what this unit of volume means.

Matching work to pupils

Matching the learning experience to the ability level, interests and needs of each pupil in the class is one of the most skilful aspects of teaching. The difficulty of doing this successfully is in part a reflection of the complexity of the teacher's task: namely, that the class may well have about 30 pupils in it, comprising a range of ability, interests and needs. Indeed, the HMI (1988b), in their observations of lessons given by probationary teachers, noted that in general, the needs of average-ability pupils were better catered for than those of above and below average ability in the class.

In part, this reflects a tendency when teaching to pitch the lesson towards meeting the needs of the broad middle range of ability within the class, and then to provide additional material, demands or help for those at the extremes. Part of the problem with this approach is that the more able pupils need more enriching and more stimulating demands, not simply more of the same or more difficult work. Similarly, less able pupils also need more enriching and stimulating demands, not simply less of the same or easier work. A number of work schemes based on individualised programmes of work have been particularly successful in enabling this match to occur across a broad range of ability. In addition, grouping pupils into narrower ability bands can also be helpful, although there is a danger here that pupils grouped together into a low-ability band may get caught up in a vicious circle of lowered teacher and pupil expectations concerning what they are capable of.

The notion of matching work to pupils does not mean setting work at a level that pupils can already do fairly successfully. Rather, it deals with the idea of what pupils of a certain level of ability are able to achieve in the way of new learning. 'Matching the work' thus refers to deciding how much progress pupils can make in a given lesson or over a course of lessons and then pitching the work to achieve the optimal progress the pupils appear to be capable of.

In a study of pupil progress in primary schools, Mortimore *et al*, (1988) noted that a key factor contributing to greater progress was intellectually challenging teaching. However, detailed analyses of the match of task demands to pupils in primary schools (Bennett *et al*, 1984) and in secondary schools (Kerry, 1984) indicate that a majority of tasks were not well-matched to pupils, in this sense of promoting the optimal progress pupils were capable of. While the study by Bennett *et al* indicated that primary school teachers often provided tasks which were either too easy or too difficult, Kerry's study indicated that secondary school teachers erred overmuch in the direction of providing too easy tasks.

Skilful matching

One of the useful ways in which teachers can help ensure that a match is ocurring is through careful monitoring of pupils' progress and questioning to check understanding. Unfortunately, many pupils are reluctant to confess to difficulties and are likely to do instead either little work in silence, or else use various strategies to get the work demanded done with little or even incorrect understanding. As such, it is of crucial importance that you take the initiative in monitoring progress, rather than wait for difficulties to be drawn to your attention.

Expectations also play a role in sometimes obscuring what pupils are capable of. Most pupils will do slightly less than is typically demanded of them. This can easily result in a downward spiral of teacher demands, if what the teacher demands of each lesson is the level of work that was produced in previous lessons. As such, you need to be consistently conveying expectations of a higher quality of work and progress each lesson than is typically achieved. This will create an impression of encouraging and expecting a standard just higher than the norm previously produced, but not so much higher that pupils feel discouraged or that you are dissatisfied with genuine effort on their part.

Matching work to pupils also concerns the need to take account of pupils' interests and needs. This includes taking advantage of examples and topics and their applications that are likely to be of interest or relevance to the pupils in your class. In addition, it includes providing a variety of ways of working, using both teacher talk activities and a range of academic tasks, so that pupils can build up the skills involved in working successfully in these different ways.

Some pupils will also have particular needs that need to be met. These may range from a pupil who is rather shy and needs encouragement to participate, to a pupil who has difficulty producing legible handwriting. Such pupils will require individual attention for their needs to be met. Some pupils may well have a marked learning difficulty and are identified as having a special educational need. In such cases, the teacher may be able to meet these needs, or else there may be additional help or resources available. Indeed, all teachers need to be alert to the possibility that a pupil may have a special educational need and to ensure that such needs are identified and met. Learning difficulties may stem from a physical handicap of some sort, a long period of absence from school, very low general ability, or social and emotional problems.

Tutoring

Another aspect of matching work to pupils is the use of one-to-one teaching, sometimes referred to as tutoring. As well as whole-class teaching and the monitoring of progress on academic tasks, teachers also spend much of their time helping individual pupils on a one-to-one basis. This type of help is a crucial part of effective teaching, not only because of the academic help offered, but also because it is a personal and private encounter between you and the pupil. As such, it offers an important opportunity to emphasize your care, support and encouragement for the pupil's progress. It also provides an important opportunity to assess the pupil's general ability and motivation, and to identify any particular needs.

The effectiveness of such tutoring has long been recognised, and some schools now make use of parents as helpers in the classroom or use other pupils, including older pupils, to provide additional opportunities for one-to-one help in the classroom. The use of pupils as tutors, often referred to as 'peer tutoring', is fairly widespread and a number of studies have indicated that where older pupils are asked to help younger pupils in this way (usually with reading or number work), both pupils seem to benefit (eg Fitz-Gibbon, 1988). Of particular importance in using other adults or pupils as tutors in this way, is that they are carefully briefed about their role and the need to offer encouragement during the interactions.

A wide variety of resources are available

Using resources and materials

There is a vast range of resources and materials available for use in the classroom, including audiotapes, videotapes, slides, overhead projector transparencies, worksheets and workcards, computer packages and simulation materials. Perhaps the golden rule concerning their use is always to check their quality and appropriateness for the lesson. It is all too easy to think that because such resources are going to be used, that is an excuse for accepting a somewhat lower quality or something not quite appropriate for the intended learning. As a result, pupils all too often have to watch videos with poor sound quality or work through a computer package that is unclear or even inappropriate to the topic being investigated. While the desire for pupils to acquire a familiarity with such materials may be important enough to warrant this on the odd occasion, you must be rigorous in your appraisal of the suitability of such materials for the learning outcomes you intend.

It is also important to familiarise yourself with the content of such materials if you have not used them before or for some time, since it may prove difficult to deal with any problems that may arise unexpectedly. In addition, since many resources may be used by pupils with little help from the teacher, difficulties may arise which you may not be aware of until after the lesson or not at all, unless you carefully monitor progress.

The blackboard

The blackboard is still the most widely used teaching aid and the quality of blackboard use will be a major indicator of the quality of your teaching. Well-prepared and clear use of the blackboard is not only effective as a teaching aid, but is also an example to the class of the standard of quality of work and presentation you expect. The blackboard can also usefully be used as a reminder or record of important points: for example, the spelling of new or difficult words, a note of the task pupils are to undertake when the present task has been completed, or a list of pupils' ideas to be used for later analysis. One pitfall for beginning teachers to note is talking while facing the blackboard. When you are writing on the board and have something to say, you must turn your head to face the class as you speak.

Similar points can be made about the use of the overhead projector, although here it is possible to produce transparencies in advance to good effect. In using the overhead projector, always ensure that the projection onto the screen is clearly visible from all parts of the classroom, and ensure that you are not obscuring the view yourself (an occasional fault, even amongst some experienced teachers!).

Individualised schemes of work

The two most marked areas of development in the use of resources and materials has been the widespread use of individualised schemes of work based on computer packages and workcards. In both cases, one of the skills involved in their effective use concerns the organisation of how and when pupils use these, and how and when they receive feedback on their progress.

Many studies have indicated that one of the key factors in promoting greater pupil attainment is the ability of the teacher to maximise the time that pupils spend educationally benefitting from the learning activity in hand. The more time they spend waiting to use resources or waiting for help when they are in difficulties, the less time they are making progress in their attainment. The procedures used by teachers to ensure good organisation in using such resources is thus of great importance.

One advantage of some computer packages and workcards is that they are designed to be self-explanatory and often provide feedback concerning correct answers and help for pupils in difficulties. Nevertheless, most such resources do still require teacher assistance from time to time, and for teachers to be involved in assessing progress. As such, you need to ensure that the arrangements you make allow such time to be given. One particularly useful strategy, commonly employed in primary schools, is to organise a lesson such that different groups are working on different tasks, ranging from tasks involving minimal teacher contact, to those involving a great deal of contact. By dividing the class up in this way, you will be able to spend more time with those pupils needing your help without this being to the detriment of other pupils. Another useful strategy is to establish routines or procedures that pupils are required to follow, so that they do not waste time wondering what to do next in a particular situation. A simple rule concerning what pupils are to do if they get into difficulties or have finished a piece of work can help to ensure smooth running of classroom activities, and enables you to check whether the activities set are causing problems, are too easy or are unclear in any respect.

Treating resources and materials with care

Finally, when resources and materials are used by pupils that are to be used again by others, it is worth emphasizing that the resources must be handled with care and respect. This is important not only because loss or damage may be costly and also inconvenience other pupils, but also because it highlights that in life everyone will be sharing resources and that such common ownership and use imposes responsibilities and obligations on each user. What is true in this respect within the community of the school, is also true for society in general.

Key questions about your lesson presentation

1 *Are the learning activities appropriate to the type of learning outcomes I intend?*

2 *Do the learning activities take adequate account of pupils' abilities, interests and needs, and of their previous and future learning?*

3 *Do I make use of a variety of different types of learning activities?*

4 *Are my instructions, explanations and questions, clear and appropriate for pupils' needs?*

5 *Do I use a variety of question types and distribute these widely throughout the class?*

6 *Is my general manner confident, relaxed, self-assured and purposeful, and one that is conducive to generating an interest in the lesson and providing support and encouragement for learning?*

7 *Does my lesson take adequate account of any particular needs of individual pupils, including any special educational needs?*

8 *Are resources and materials used to good effect?*

9 *Do I carefully monitor the progress of the lesson and the progress of pupils' learning to ensure that the learning activities are effectively fostering the learning outcomes I intend?*

10 *Does my general standard of presentation indicate to pupils my respect and care for their learning?*

4 Lesson management

Teaching a class of 30 pupils requires a whole range of management and organisational skills if sufficient order necessary for pupil learning is to occur. In many ways, I think the task of teaching is rather like the act one sometimes sees on a stage where a person has to spin plates on top of several canes simultaneously. To do this successfully requires the performer to set new plates spinning while occasionally returning to those plates that have slowed down and are near to falling off, for a booster spin. In the same way, successful lesson management requires you to keep switching your attention and action between several activities to ensure that pupils' learning proceeds smoothly.

The key task facing you as a teacher is to elicit and sustain pupils' involvement in a learning experience throughout a lesson which will lead to the learning outcomes you intend. At any one time you are likely to have several demands pressing on you for action. For example, you may be dealing with a pupil having problems with the task in hand, then become aware that another pupil needs an item of equipment, also notice another pupil is staring out of the window apparently daydreaming, and be approached by another pupil who wants some work checked.

Lesson management essentially refers to those skills involved in managing and organising the learning activities such that you maximise pupils' productive involvement in the lesson as much as possible. Given the large size and range of ability of most classes, this is no mean task! Research based on classroom observation and interviews with beginning and experienced teachers has identified just how a successful lesson hinges on some key skills.

Paradoxically, watching successful experienced teachers in action tends to provide student teachers with little explicit guidance on successful lesson management skills, since such teachers make everything look too easy. It is only when such teaching is contrasted with that of teachers where problems arise, that the difference in what they do becomes evident, and the skills used by successful lesson managers can be described.

Beginnings, transitions and endings

One of the key areas of lesson management concerns the skills used in beginning a lesson, handling the transitions within the lesson between activities (say, moving from group work to classroom discussion) and bringing a lesson to a successful ending.

Beginning punctually

The two most important aspects concerning the beginning of the lesson are punctuality and mental set. Punctuality refers to the importance of the lesson starting fairly soon after the time formally timetabled for its start. This requires that both you and your pupils have arrived for the lesson in good time. Ideally, it is a great help if you can be in the classroom first, to greet pupils as they arrive and to ensure that pupils enter the classroom in an orderly fashion and settle down quickly. Certainly you should convey to pupils that lateness is not acceptable without a good excuse.

For the first few minutes of a lesson, there is usually a period of dead time during which pupils settle down, books may be distributed, or you may check material or notes. If possible, you can usually use this time to good effect by having a social exchange with one or two pupils, or deal with some matter outstanding from a previous lesson, such as a pupil's overdue homework. Once you are happy that everyone has arrived, you need to signal that the lesson itself is ready to begin. This is probably the most important moment in the lesson. It signals the moment that pupils are to pay attention and begin their involvement in the lesson. A clear explicit signal, perhaps saying 'Righto everyone' or 'Pay attention now', is required. It is immensely important for pupils to start paying attention immediately. If you are not happy that all pupils are paying attention, you should indicate this. Trying to continue with the start of a lesson when a few pupils are not paying attention often acts as a signal for others to do likewise in future.

Establishing a positive mental set

Most lessons begin with the topic in hand or with some short activity that needs to be dealt with first, such as comments on homework, or some comment about equipment or materials that everyone should have ready. Whether you start with the topic itself or some other activity, it is important to stand centre-stage, at the front of the room, and use a clear voice, eye contact and scanning, to ensure that everyone is paying attention. A pause followed by a stare at someone not paying attention is often sufficient to signal this.

Once you begin to introduce the topic in hand for the lesson, you need to think about how to elicit and sustain pupils' interest. The best way to do this is to convey in your tone of voice and general manner, a sense of curiosity and excitement, and a sense of purposefulness about what is to follow. Two useful techniques are to establish a link with previous work (eg 'Now you remember last week we looked at ...') or to pose some questions (eg 'Can anybody tell me what the word energy means?'). Such techniques help to establish a positive mental set towards the lesson, *viz* an attitude of mind in which the pupil prepares to devote attention and mental effort towards the activities you set up. A successful introduction to a lesson, which establishes a positive mental set, makes it far easier to sustain learning as the lesson unfolds.

Another aspect of establishing this mental set is to check that every pupil is ready and prepared for the start of the lesson. Are there still pupils with bags on the desk, or standing up talking to each other, or looking for an exercise book that was not handed back? One of the skills involved here is deciding whether to hold up the start of the lesson and chivvy pupils to settle down quickly (eg 'Hurry up now, I can still see two bags on desks') or whether simply by starting, pupils will quickly pay attention.

Once a routine for a quick and smooth start to lessons has been well-established, you can normally relax the formality of the start, as pupils will quickly respond. However, it is useful from time to time to re-emphasize the procedure and expectations to ensure that they continue to operate well. At the same time, you also need to check that you are ready and prepared for the start of the lesson. Are the materials you intend to use readily to hand, has a diagram you wish them to talk about been drawn on the board, are the copies of the worksheet to be used ready for distribution? A state of readiness on your part will contribute to your own mental set.

Smooth transitions

The notion of 'smoothness' is helpful when considering whether a lesson has started smoothly and whether there has been a smooth transition between activities. This can best be described by contrasting it with the notion of 'jerkiness'. Jerkiness would be evident if the teacher had to repeat instructions because pupils had not heard or were confused by what was said, or if the teacher had to keep referring back to earlier points because something had been omitted or needed clarifying.

For example, having told pupils to start working through a worksheet, the teacher may interrupt the work ten minutes later to say that the first three questions can only be answered with the information in their textbook. This not only interrupts the pupils, but may even mean their earlier efforts had been misguided or unproductive. The worst form of jerkiness would be attempting to start an activity only to find that some prior activity needed to be undertaken first, and as a result needing to stop the activity and change to the prior activity. Effective beginnings and transitions are smooth in the sense of lacking jerkiness. Clearly, from time to time, such jerkiness is required for good educational reasons, such as if it becomes evident that an unforeseeable learning difficulty has arisen. Nevertheless, skilful teaching tends to be characterised by a minimum of unnecessary and avoidable instances of jerkiness.

In looking at smooth transitions, two other aspects of transitions contribute to smoothness. First, the teacher needs to be sensitive to how a lesson is progressing in deciding when to initiate a transition. For example, if pupils seem to be working fairly well at a task but somewhat slower than anticipated, the teacher may well decide that it is better to allow more time for the task to continue, rather than interrupt the activity before it is completed to move them on to another activity. In some cases this may be crucial. A transition to discussion following group work may be harder to set up effectively if the group work had not continued long enough for the issues or ideas to develop that were to form the basis for the discussion.

The second aspect of transitions worthy of note is deciding when to give instructions to the class as a whole, rather than to individuals. All too often a teacher interrupts a class embarking on a new activity simply to issue a further or elaborated instruction which is only of use to two or three particular pupils. It may well have been better and less disruptive for the teacher to talk to each of those pupils privately. The same pitfall can relate to issuing a reprimand, which again may disrupt the working of the whole class when simple and silent eye contact might have been more effective and less disruptive.

The key point to bear in mind concerning transitions is that care and attention to setting up a sequence of activities in which pupils are working steadily and well is just as important as the effort you put into dealing with the content of the learning activities.

Ending the lesson

The ending of lessons can usefully include a few words of praise concerning the work covered and some conclusions or summary about what was achieved. Three important issues of management concern endings. First, a lesson should end on time, neither early, nor, except for special reasons, late. Good time management is one of the skills that pupils will fairly expect you to have. Ending early can imply a lack of concern about the worthwhileness of using all the time available. Should some time be available at the end of a lesson, this time can be usefully spent recapping or probing the topic covered. Ending late can imply that you lack the organisational skills to marshall the activities together, and will deprive you of the opportunity to finish the lesson in a well-ordered and unhurried fashion. Most pupils will naturally resent lessons running over time on a regular basis.

A second management issue concerns the procedure for getting pupils ready for the end of the lesson. This may involve collecting books and equipment, giving feedback on the work done, and setting homework or other action needed before the next lesson. While this should occur in good time, you also need to ensure that some pupils do not start to pack away too early or before you have signalled this.

Third, the exit from the classroom should be well-ordered. If necessary, it should be controlled, with you dismissing groups of pupils at a time, rather than allowing a rushed exit, until such time as pupils are used to making a well-ordered exit from the classroom without your explicit control.

Maintaining pupils' involvement

Once the lesson is underway, your main task is to maintain pupils' attention, interest and involvement in the learning activities. The task is *not*, however, one of simply keeping pupils busy. There may be a number of activities that you could set up that would effectively keep pupils busy, but they may not be effectively promoting the learning you intend. What makes lesson management skills so sophisticated is the task of setting up activities that are both educationally effective and maintain pupils' involvement.

While the two should go together, it is easy to find some activities erring too far towards only the latter. Skilful lesson management is primarily a question of getting a good balance between the learning potential of an activity and its degree of sustaining pupils' involvement. Since learning cannot occur without involvement, a danger facing teachers is to be uncritical about the quality of learning which occurs when they have successfully maintained a high level of pupil involvement. Nevertheless, at the same time, one needs to bear in mind that the learning outcomes which teachers try to achieve include the development of study skills, organisational skills and sustained concentration by pupils. These can usefully be fostered by lengthy periods of working without interaction with the teacher. As such, a teacher may well choose to use an activity which can sustain high pupil involvement for a long period primarily as a means to foster such skills.

Monitoring pupils' progress

Overall, the most important skill involved in maintaining pupils' involvement is that of careful monitoring of pupils' progress. This should be done actively, through circulating around the room and asking probing questions, and passively, by having well-established routines whereby pupils are encouraged to ask for help. Both active and passive monitoring is important. As a result of such monitoring, key decisions are made about how best to sustain pupils' involvement. Such decisions may relate to the needs of one or two particular pupils or to the needs of the class as a whole.

Pace and flow of the lesson

If pupils' attention or interest in the lesson seems to be on the wane, a number of possible reasons may account for this. It may be that a particular activity is being employed for too long (most commonly a too long exposition). Alternatively, it may be that the general pace and flow of the lesson is either too fast or too slow.

If the pace of activities (be it exposition, group work, worksheets or reading tasks) is too fast, pupils will simply wilt or find that they are losing important points or ideas. If the pace is too slow, pupils' minds can easily start to wander. Indeed, an important aspect of maintaining the correct pace during exposition involves having a sense of how long to dwell on each particular point for understanding to occur, and not spending too long dwelling on minor points or points already well taken.

In addition, maintaining a good pace also involves avoiding unnecessary interruptions to the flow of the lesson. For example, if while explaining a task, you stop in order to get a pencil for a pupil, or to find a map you need to refer to, or to reprimand a pupil, the flow of the lesson will be interrupted. A useful lesson management skill is that of dealing with demands that arise, or postponing dealing with them, so that they are not allowed to interrupt the flow of the lesson. For example, if while explaining a task you notice two pupils talking, you may continue your explanation while looking at the two pupils concerned, or, if necessary, move towards them. This would enable the flow of the lesson to continue while dealing with the problem. This skill is sometimes referred to as 'overlapping', *viz* dealing with two or more tasks at the same time.

Another example of overlapping is the teacher's ability to monitor pupils' progress and behaviour while giving individual help to a particular pupil. A skilful teacher is able to listen to a pupil reading aloud or give help with some number work, for example, while at the same time periodically scanning the classroom and listening to the background noise, to pick out any behaviour giving concern. This involves quickly switching attention between your interaction with the particular pupil and what else is going on in the classroom. Indeed, a particular pitfall for beginning teachers is to become so engrossed in giving individual help and attention, so as to fail to monitor what else is happening. An experienced teacher can do this, and more!

You have to be able to do a wide variety of things at the same time

Withitness

The general awareness of what is going on in the classroom is commonly referred to as 'withitness'. Experienced teachers are adept at picking up cues and signals which indicate to them what is going on. A quick downward glance by a pupil in the back row, or a furtive look at a neighbour, or simply taking slightly too long to walk to a seat, can all be picked up by a teacher as signalling the onset of possible misbehaviour.

Beginning teachers are often so overwhelmed by all the demands of classroom life that they find it difficult to pick up such signals. With increasing experience, which gradually makes the unfamiliar familiar, the teacher becomes better able to pick up and monitor subtle cues of this type. As such, it is useful for beginning teachers to consciously make an effort to scan the classroom periodically and monitor general behaviour, to see if anything gives concern. It is also useful to bear in mind the times when such monitoring is vulnerable. As well as when giving individual help, times when your back is turned to the classroom while writing on the board or looking in cupboards may interrupt your monitoring. A useful technique when writing on the board is to face sideways or to glance back at the class regularly.

Interestingly, the importance of lesson management skills concerning transitions, overlapping and withitness, was highlighted in a study by Kounin (1970), in which he compared the videotaped classroom behaviour of teachers who were regarded as having few discipline problems with teachers having frequent problems. What was particularly notable was that the former's relative success largely stemmed from them being simply more effective lesson managers, rather than anything to do with how they dealt with pupil misbehaviour itself. Research on teaching skills, including my own (eg Kyriacou and McKelvey, 1985), indicates that experienced teachers are generally skilful in these three important aspects of their classroom practice.

Managing pupils' time

Pupils' involvement in the lesson can also be facilitated if pupils are given a clear idea of how much time and effort they are expected to devote to particular tasks or activities. For example, if you ask pupils to copy a map into their exercise books and answer three questions related to the map, some pupils may rush the task anticipating that ten minutes should be sufficient time, and others may assume the task is intended to last half-an-hour. If you indicate that the task should take about 20 minutes, it will help pupils to tailor their effort to the time available.

This can of course sometimes be a danger, in encouraging pupils to perhaps take longer than they need. In general, however, it helps to ensure that some pupils do not work slowly only to find they are half-way through the task when you want pupils to move on to another activity. It also helps pupils to maintain attention and interest, since they have a clear sense that another activity is shortly to follow. This helps to break the lesson up into more attractive chunks of time.

Giving supportive feedback

Constructive and helpful feedback also needs to be given to pupils to support and encourage further progress. Such feedback is not only of practical use to pupils in identifying problems or indicating successful work, but also conveys to pupils that their progress is being carefully monitored and that you care about such progress. Such regular feedback thus offers a periodic boost to their motivation and effort.

The skill of offering such feedback is a fairly complex one that needs time and practice to develop. You need to be able to identify the nature of the pupil's problem. Simply indicating a 'correct' method may not be enough to give the pupil the insight necessary. You also need to be able to offer feedback in a way that is unthreatening, since once a pupil feels anxious, it is harder for the pupil to follow what is being said. This requires the use of a sympathetic tone of voice, and identifying the problem in the task or activity, rather than in the pupil. In other words, it is better to say 'In this type of question, it is useful to make a note of the information given in the diagram', rather than 'You should have been more careful in your approach'. The former statement is task-focused, whereas the latter locates the fault or blame with the pupil. This sensitivity to pupils' feelings is now widely appreciated as being an important aspect of the skill involved in providing supportive feedback. Indeed, in a survey of secondary school pupils' attitudes, Branwhite (1988) reported that the teacher's capacity to empathize was the most valued teacher quality cited by the pupils.

Giving individual feedback privately to each pupil in a fairly large class is clearly going to be demanding, and attempting to do this will almost certainly distract you from other important tasks. As such, you need to maintain a good balance between giving individual feedback and other strategies, including feedback to the whole class, or enabling pupils to correct their own or each other's work. These other techniques help to ensure that feedback occurs regularly and with sufficient speed to improve the quality of work and learning. However, you do need to ensure that such techniques are used sensitively, given the emotional consequences of identifying failure.

Adjusting your lesson plans

Careful monitoring of pupils' progress and giving feedback also enables you to consider how best the lesson ought to proceed in the light of its success to date and any problems encountered. While lesson plans are important, all teachers will need to tailor the development of the lesson to the needs of the moment. As such, part of successful lesson management involves making whatever adjustments to your original plans for the lesson are necessary. In doing so, however, always ensure that you have a good feel as to how the class as a whole is progressing. Clearly, just because one or two pupils are finding the work too easy or too difficult or lacking interest, this should not be taken as a signal that this is generally true for most of the class. Once you get to know a class fairly well, however, it becomes possible to make useful inferences from the behaviour of just a handful of pupils. If, for example, two or three pupils who normally find the work in hand difficult are suddenly racing through a particular task, you may well be fairly certain that most pupils in the class are going to complete the task quickly without the need for you to check too widely for confirmation.

Handling the logistics of classroom life

Lesson management skills are essential if the learning activities you set up are to take place with sufficient order for learning to occur. Almost any task or activity can lead to chaos unless you give some thought to the organisation of how and when pupils are to do what is required of them. Organised control over the logistics of classroom life, whether it be how pupils answer questions, collect equipment from cupboards, or form themselves into small groups, requires explicit direction from you, at least until the procedures you expect are followed as a matter of routine.

Social demand tasks

In a study of teachers' management effectiveness, Weade and Evertson (1988) argued that every learning activity involves a 'social demand task'. This social demand task concerns, for example, who can talk to whom, about what, where, when, in what ways and for what purpose? Their findings, based on classroom observation, served to highlight the importance of how teachers indicate to pupils what is required of them, and facilitate the smooth and effective running of the activity. Indeed, with the increasing variety of learning activities used, ranging from small group work to role-play exercises, effective lesson management skills need to be applied to a host of very different types of activities to deal with the social demand task involved in each.

The handling of pupil talk in the classroom demands particular control, whether it be as part of classroom discussion channelled through the teacher, or as part of exchanges between two pupils working together. As part of classroom discussion, it is essential to ensure that only one pupil speaks at a time and is heard by others. The simplest way to organise this is to insist that each pupil who wishes to speak must first raise a hand. Such a formalised ritual can be relaxed to some extent, but if it is, you must take care that certain pupils are not disadvantaged from making contributions. It is also useful to make sure that other pupils can hear what is said, either by getting the pupil to speak louder or by repeating or paraphrasing what was said yourself (the former is preferrable, but particular circumstances may make the latter more appropriate). You also need to be firm about not allowing background noise or conversation to build up during classroom discussion.

Group work

Setting up group work activities involves a number of decisions about the logistics of their organisation. First, there is the question of the size of the group and how groups are to be formed. If you have a task which, ideally, involves four pupils, you need to think about how the groups of four are to be created, and what to do if there are one or more pupils left over, or indeed, one or two pupils that no one wants in their group.

A second question concerns the nature of the task. Is it clear exactly what the task involves, who will undertake which roles, and how and what is to be produced? A clear instruction, such as 'At the end, each group will give a list of the four most important factors involved, in order of importance', is clearer than simply getting each group to discuss the factors involved. Often, it is useful to write the task on the board or on a briefing handout issued to each pupil or group. You may wish to let each group decide who should report back at the end, or name a pupil from each group to do this (the latter is useful in ensuring that certain pupils are given the experience of doing this).

A third aspect of group work concerns your monitoring role. While close monitoring is usually desirable, particularly in checking that everyone is clear about the task, your presence may have an inhibiting effect on group discussion, and, as such, it is often better to spend only a short while with each group to check that everything is in order, rather than to sit in for any length of time.

Fourth, clear time management directions are crucial to most group work activities. Not only is it useful to say how long each group has for the task as a whole, but also how much time they may spend on any stages that make up the task. One last aspect concerning group work is the need to help pupils develop the skills involved in successful group work. Pupils need to develop a number of skills to use group work to good effect, and feedback and guidance from you concerning good practice can help such skills to develop.

Practicals

Practicals of any sort present a number of logistical problems, in part because you need to co-ordinate your management of pupils and materials with the sequence and speed of the practical itself. In a science practical, for example, there may be a 20 minute period during which some effect is developing, when pupils may have nothing to do. Clear guidance that during this period they are to draw the apparatus used and describe the method, allows this demand to be co-ordinated with the practical to good effect.

Another common problem regarding practicals may arise if certain equipment needs to be shared. Again, a strict rota for the use of such equipment or a procedure to ensure its speedy use and return, can make a large difference to reducing unproductive time. During practicals, there are often times when bottlenecks can occur, such as when everyone wants to collect or return equipment, or perhaps wash apparatus. Simple rules, such as only allowing one pupil from each group to collect apparatus, can help prevent problems occurring.

Computer packages

Unless you have quite a few computers available for use at the same time, you need to organise a rota of some sort to ensure that all pupils use the package required in turn. In primary schools, this is not a problem as it is commonplace to have different groups working on different tasks at the same time, although it is extremely helpful if another teacher or a parent helper can be used to give specific help with the computer-based activity. In secondary schools, a shortage of computers poses more problems. Some schools, however, have successfully created resource areas which contain computers to which small groups of pupils can be sent on a rota basis to use packages with well-prepared guides for their use.

One point about pairs, or occasionally a small group of three pupils, working on computer packages, is that it is useful in most cases to group together pupils of similar ability, unless you explicitly wish one pupil to act as tutor. With other types of group work, friendship groupings seem to work well, unless there is a clear educational rationale for forming the groups on the basis of similar ability or in some other way.

Managing pupil movement and noise

Two of the most important aspects of effective management skills concern maintaining adequate control over the movement of pupils around the classroom and keeping the degree of noise generated at an appropriate level. In both cases, part of the difficulty lies in there being no fixed acceptable standard – what may be acceptable by one teacher in one context may not be regarded as acceptable to another teacher in another context. Furthermore, problems over movement and noise can arise simply as a result of pupils being actively engaged in the tasks at

Managing pupils' movement

hand and not because of any deliberate attempt by pupils to be troublesome.

Pupil movement

We have already touched on some aspects of pupil movement in the classroom earlier in this chapter, such as entering and leaving the room, and collecting equipment. In addition to these, there are some occasions which require particular attention. The first of these involves giving out books at the start of or during the lesson. It is certainly important to issue books rather than allow pupils to collect them from a central point. Often it is more efficient for you to ask two or three pupils to issue books, rather than do it yourself, unless you feel that distributing books yourself will provide a useful social function or enable you to have a few pertinent words with some pupils. If pupils are issuing the books, ensure that they do so sensibly and with care.

The second aspect concerns any mass movement of pupils; this always requires careful control. While useful routines can be established, there are occasions when you need to organise a somewhat unusual or novel arrangement. For example, you may wish to devise a role-play activity which requires all the classroom furniture, apart from eight chairs, to be moved towards the edge of the classroom. Any complicated manoeuvre of this sort requires prior thought if it is to proceed smoothly. A clear sequence of tasks and who needs to do what is essential.

The third aspect involves establishing your expectations concerning when pupils may leave their seat. Despite new forms of teaching and learning, most pupils will spend the majority of their time in their seats. Management of pupils being out of their seat during periods of work when pupils are expected to work at their desk is important. The normal expectation during such activities is that pupils remain at their desk until given explicit permission to move, unless certain well-established routines allowing movement without explicit permission are followed. In such circumstances it is useful to ensure that only a handful of pupils at any one time are out of their seats, or away from their work area; it becomes much harder to monitor pupils' progress if several pupils appear to be wandering about, even if their purposes are legitimate. This is one reason why teachers often set an upper limit on how many pupils are allowed to queue up at the teacher's desk. Being out of one's seat for some pupils also acts as a break from their work, and they may feel like extending this break longer than necessary, and may also, as a result, start to disturb others. This needs careful monitoring.

Pupil noise

Managing the general level of noise is also an important management skill. Every teacher develops their own standard of acceptable level of noise. The key thing here is to be reasonably consistent, so that pupils have a clear idea of your expectations. If the level of background noise during an activity appears to be too high, it is useful to give specific feedback on the work practice you require, rather than a general complaint that the noise is too high. Thus, for example, it is better to say 'You can talk to your neighbour, but not to other pupils' or 'Try to ensure that only one person in each group is speaking at a time' is better than simply saying 'The noise level is too high' or 'Less noise please'.

It is also worth planning the activities to ensure that noise levels are not disruptive. For example, in a science practical looking at sound as a form of energy, clear instructions on how the apparatus or equipment is to be used can prevent problems occurring through unnecessarily high noise levels. Indeed, the opportunity to make a lot of noise legitimately is too tempting for many pupils to resist. At the same time, it must be recognised that a certain level of noise is, of course, acceptable and desirable, and that enthusiastic and excited contributions by pupils need to be harnessed to good effect rather than squashed. Clearly, a balance that ensures sufficient order is what is needed.

Some studies, however, have indicated that the teacher's management of noise can sometimes become an end in itself. Given that the noise level of a class is often taken as an indicator of the teacher's level of control, many teachers are very sensitive about their classroom noise level, particularly if they feel it may be heard by colleagues or interfere with colleagues' lessons. A study by Denscombe (1980) argued that beginning teachers felt under particular pressure to control the noise level of their classes lest it conveyed to colleagues that they lacked control. As a result, teachers may sometimes use a learning activity in part because it will enable a sustained period of quiet work by pupils to take place, even if another activity more effective for the learning outcomes intended might have been used instead. Some of the reluctance by some teachers to make greater use of group work is related to the greater level of noise such activity typically generates.

Movement and noise as constraints on your teaching

While the management of movement and noise is important, you do need to be on your guard concerning whether, as indicated above, you are allowing management considerations to have too great an influence on your choice of effective learning activities. Skilful lesson management involves an interplay between the different constraints within which you operate. Clearly, you need to ensure that a role-play activity involving a lot of movement and noise does not disturb another class, or that one pupil's excitement does not lead to other pupils being constantly interrupted when they are speaking. At the same time, you need to ensure that the learning activity does facilitate and encourage pupils' attention, interest and involvement in the lesson, and that this is not unduly inhibited by management strategies that could be usefully relaxed to good effect.

One of the dilemmas facing teachers is that they may feel better able to manage certain types of lessons, and as a result are reluctant to use other types of learning activities. This results in them not gaining the experience to develop the new management skills needed. For example, in a survey of how mathematics teachers are developing new approaches to their teaching, many heads of departments reported difficulties arising from the reluctance of some colleagues to develop new approaches that they felt were outside their expertise, despite the fact that certain curriculum developments had made the need for such change essential (Kyriacou, 1990).

In thinking about your own classroom practice, you should not be wary of setting up activities that may involve more than usual movement or noise, as long as this is well-managed and to good purpose. Some years ago a well-known headteacher remarked that effective teaching could sometimes be described as 'organised chaos'. I think that there is some truth in this description in so far as an observer of a lesson may well feel that so many activities were occurring that a degree of close teacher supervision, monitoring and control was being lost. Some effective lessons may well appear to have such a quality. Nevertheless, you must be aware of the need to retain sufficient order and control for effective learning to occur. There can at times be a danger in thinking that certain activities are so worthwhile in their own right, particularly in terms of the extent to which they may offer pupils a fair measure of control over their own work, that the need to maintain sufficient order and control for effective learning can be relaxed. While I am a strong advocate of using a variety of learning activities, particularly active learning methods, there is always a need to ensure that effective learning is occurring, and to provide the conditions that will facilitate this. Again, what is required here is an appropriate balance between the management strategies used and the type of learning outcomes you intend, most notably if the learning outcomes are in terms of developing the pupils' own skills to organise themselves.

Key questions about your lesson management

1 *Does my lesson start smoothly and promptly, and induce a positive mental set among pupils?*

2 *Does the management of the lesson help to elicit and maintain pupils' attention, interest and motivation?*

3 *Is the pace and flow of the lesson maintained at an appropriate level and are transitions between activities well-managed?*

4 *Do I carefully monitor the progress of pupils so that the effectiveness of the lesson is maintained by giving individual help or making modifications and adjustments to the development of the lesson, as appropriate?*

5 *Do I give clear guidance and direction concerning what is expected of pupils during each activity, and manage their time and effort, in relation to their involvement in and the sequencing of the various activities, to good effect?*

6 *Do I make effective use of the various materials, resources and teaching aids, so that pupils' time is not wasted waiting for equipment to be set up or materials distributed?*

7 *Do I organise and control the logistics of classroom life, such as how pupils answer questions, collect equipment, or form into groups, so that the order necessary for learning to occur is maintained?*

8 *In particular, do I use effective management strategies in handling pupil movement and the general level of noise?*

9 *Is the feedback conveyed to pupils about their progress helpful and constructive, and does it encourage further progress?*

10 *Do my lessons end effectively, in terms of ending on time, drawing the topic of the lesson to an appropriate conclusion, and having a well-ordered exit by pupils from the classroom?*

5 Classroom climate

Establishing a positive classroom climate

The classroom climate established by the teacher can have a major impact on pupils' motivation and attitude towards learning. As such, the skills involved in establishing a positive classroom climate are of immense importance.

The type of classroom climate generally considered to best facilitate pupil learning is one that is described as being purposeful, task-oriented, relaxed, warm, supportive and has a sense of order. Such a climate facilitates learning, in essence, by establishing and maintaining positive attitudes and motivation by pupils towards the lesson. In analysing the skills involved in setting up a positive classroom climate, it is clear that the climate largely derives from the values that are implicit and pervade the lesson – simply that pupils and their learning are of immense importance.

Purposeful and task-oriented
A purposeful and task-oriented ethos stems largely from the way in which the teacher emphasizes the need to make steady progress with the learning in hand. An important aspect of this derives from your insistence that time must not be wasted. Hence, a prompt start to the lesson, close monitoring of pupils' progress, and careful attention to organisational matters, all help to ensure a smooth flow to the lesson and maintenance of pupil involvement. Where teachers allow minor matters or avoidable organisational problems to interrupt the flow of the lesson, a message is conveyed to pupils that the learning is not of such immense importance that it warranted more care to ensure that it was not interrupted. Certainly, conveying in your tone of voice or even worse, adding as a preamble to a topic that it is not particularly worthwhile, will undermine creating a purposeful and task-oriented ethos. Ending a lesson early is likely to have the same effect.

Overall, a purposeful and task-oriented emphasis can usefully be described as a 'business-like' style of presentation. This is characterised by the pupils' acceptance of the teacher's authority to organise and manage the learning activities, and a pervading expectation by the teacher and pupils that a positive effort will be made by pupils to undertake the work in hand and that good progress will be made.

A very important aspect of establishing such positive expectations by pupils, is the need to ensure that pupils have self-respect and self-esteem regarding themselves as learners. This can, in part, be fostered by providing realistic opportunities for success, and helpful support and encouragement whenever pupils experience difficulties. Learning is an emotionally high-risk activity and failure is often extremely painful. Prolonged experience of failure or deprecating remarks by a teacher about pupils' low attainment can have devastating consequences for pupils' self-esteem. As a result, quite naturally, such pupils are likely to withdraw from making further efforts as a means of protecting themselves from further pain (in effect, if I am not trying, my lack of success is simply my choice).

Relaxed, warm and supportive

A relaxed, warm and supportive ethos stems largely from the style and manner of the relationship you establish with the pupils. Being relaxed yourself, and in particular, dealing with any pupil misbehaviour calmly, helps pupils to relax too. This better enables pupils to develop curiosity and interest in the learning activities.

Warmth can best be thought of as conveying to pupils a sense that you care for them and their learning personally, partly out of your affection for them as individuals. This is conveyed in the way you deal with individual pupils. Simply saying at the end of giving individual help, 'Have you got that now?' in a sympathetic and caring tone of voice, can do much to convey this sense of warmth. Pye (1988), in his analysis of skilful teaching, used the phrase 'solicitous tenderness' to describe the mixture of warmth, reassurance, kindness and tact shown by skilful teachers in how they handle interactions with pupils.

Being supportive refers to the efforts you make to help and encourage pupils to meet the demands made on them and, in particular, to deal with difficulties they encounter in a situation where they need further assistance rather than being admonished. However, you do need to be aware of the fact that too readily providing individual help and support may encourage some pupils to rely on such help rather than to make the appropriate effort to pay attention during whole class teaching or to work things out for themselves. In giving supportive feedback, you can usefully help pupils to develop study skills by indicating how paying attention earlier or using certain strategies in approaching their work will enable them to meet the demands made on them. In the context of establishing a positive classroom climate, such feedback can be a useful part of offering support.

A sense of order

The final aspect of a positive classroom climate is the need to establish a sense of order. Clearly, a sense of order can be established in many different ways. What is advocated here, is that to contribute to a positive classroom climate, suich order needs to arise out of and complement the other features considered in establishing a purposeful, task-oriented, relaxed, warm and supportive ethos. Such order will thus be based on effective lesson presentation and lesson management skills and on a relationship with pupils based on mutual respect and rapport.

Studies of classroom climate

A number of major studies looking at effective teaching and effective schools have focused on the notion of climate or ethos (eg the study of London primary schools by Mortimore *et al.* (1988) and the study of London secondary schools by Rutter *et al.* (1979)). Such studies have provided a wealth of evidence to support the importance of a positive classroom climate in facilitating pupil learning, and are in line with the judgements expressed in a series of influential HMI reports dealing with aspects of skilful teaching and good classroom practice (eg HMI, 1988a, b).

Interestingly, a number of studies have noted how important the first few lessons with a new class are in establishing a positive classroom climate. Wragg and Wood (1984), for example, compared experienced teachers with student teachers, and noted that experienced teachers:

- were more confident, warm and friendly
- were more business-like
- were more stimulating
- were more mobile
- made greater use of eye contact
- made greater use of humour
- were clearer about their classroom rules
- better established their presence and authority.

These are all features which helped them to establish fairly quickly a working climate for the school year ahead.

Motivating pupils

An essential feature of the teaching skills involved in establishing a positive classroom climate concerns how best to foster pupils' motivation towards learning. In looking at pupil motivation, a useful distinction can be made between three major influences on pupil motivation in the classroom:

- intrinsic motivation
- extrinsic motivation
- expectation for success.

Influences on pupil motivation

Intrinsic motivation concerns the extent to which pupils engage in an activity in order to satisfy their curiosity and interest in the topic area being covered or develop their competence and skills in dealing with the demands made on them, *for their own sake*. All human beings appear to have a natural drive of curiosity and wish to develop competence and skills in various tasks for their own sake, rather than as a means to some other end.

Extrinsic motivation involves engaging in an activity in order to achieve some end or goal which is rewarding and is external to the task itself. Engaging in the activity is thus a means towards some other end (eg getting praise from parents or the teacher, an academic qualification, eliciting respect and admiration from fellow pupils, or avoiding some unpleasant consequences of being unsuccessful). Intrinsic and extrinsic motivation are often contrasted with each other, but are not in fact incompatible. Indeed, many pupils have high intrinsic and high extrinsic motivation for engaging in a particular task. For example, they may work hard in their mathematics lessons both because they enjoy doing mathematics and because it is important for them to attain well in order to realise their career aspirations.

Expectation for success concerns the extent to which pupils feel they are likely to succeed at a particular activity. Most pupils will not attempt to make strenuous efforts to succeed at a task they feel is far too difficult for them and which they feel they therefore have little hope of succeeding with. Interestingly, however, not all tasks which pupils feel they can easily succeed at may be motivating; tasks that are far too easy may be seen by pupils as not being worthwhile of their effort unless there is some explicit reason to do so. Research evidence indicates that the tasks which best elicit pupil motivation are those seen by pupils to be challenging, *viz* difficult but reachable (see Good and Brophy, 1987).

Eliciting pupil motivation

The key strategies which teachers can use to elicit pupil motivation are thus concerned with building upon pupils' intrinsic motivation, extrinsic motivation and their expectation for success (see Good and Brophy, 1987). It is important to note, however, that there are large individual differences between pupils in how and when their intrinsic motivation, extrinsic motivation and expectation for success are elicited.

To a great extent these will be influenced by their experience at home (particularly how much encouragement they receive from parents to be interested in and value school learning and school-related attainment), by their experience at school (particularly their experience of success and failure to date), and how they perceive teachers' expecta-

Eliciting pupils' motivation

tions of them and the demands of various tasks. In the context of skilful teaching, the most important factor is to ensure that pupils are supported and encouraged to learn, with high positive expectations being conveyed by the teacher. Such expectations need to be realistic but challenging; they need to convey that the activities are worthwhile and of interest, and, above all, they need to convey that each pupil's progress really does matter.

Building on intrinsic motivation

Strategies which build on pupils' intrinsic motivation include selecting topics that are likely to interest pupils, particularly if they relate to pupils' own experiences. For example, charts could be based on how pupils in the class travelled to school that morning.

Offering choice can also elicit interest. For example, in composing a school newspaper, those interested in sports could compile the sports page. Active involvement and co-operation between pupils also fosters enjoyment. The use of various games has much to offer. Novelty and variety also provides a more stimulating experience. For example, starting a lesson off by producing a shoe box which purports to contain the belongings of someone found dead after a car accident, and then trying to build up as much information about the person as possible from the belongings found, would do this effectively.

Because intrinsic motivation involves a drive towards increasing competence, as well as a curiosity drive, it can be fostered by providing pupils with regular feedback concerning how their skills and competence are developing, and drawing to their attention what they can do and understand now compared with before the course of work began.

Building on extrinsic motivation

Strategies which build on pupils' extrinsic motivation include linking effort and success to material rewards and privileges. You must be extremely careful, however, to ensure that the reward or privilege offered is actually one desired by the pupils concerned and does not undermine their intrinsic motivation or alienate those who make an effort but who are not rewarded in this way. For example, offering the opportunity to those who work hard to start their playtime early, seems to devalue the worthwhileness of the activity; offering a book token to the best piece of project work may again offer far more hurt to those unsuccessful than pleasure to the pupil who wins it.

Other strategies include esteem-related rewards, such as high grades in a subject or other forms of recognition for effort or success, although, again, if such rewards are overtly competitive, you need to be cautious about their effect on other pupils. Teacher praise is a very important and powerful motivator, although its effect depends on skilful use. Praise which is explicity linked to the pupil's effort and attainment, which conveys sincere pleasure on the teacher's part, and which is used with credibility, is more effective than praise simply offered on a regular basis but lacking these qualities.

Extrinsic motivation can also be highlighted by indicating to pupils the usefulness, relevance and importance of the topic or activity to their needs. These may be their short-term needs, such as for academic qualifications or high test scores of attainment, or their long-term needs, such as coping with the demands of adult life successfully or to help realise their career aspirations.

Building on expectation for success

Strategies which build upon pupils' expectation for success include ensuring that the tasks set are challenging and offer pupils a realistic chance of success, taking into account their ability and previous learning. In particular, you need to try to minimise any unnecessary frustration caused by setting up the activities poorly. This requires close monitoring of pupils' progress once the lesson is underway, together with quick and supportive feedback when a pupil has encountered major difficulties.

Your help and expectations must convey confidence in the pupils and your belief that with appropriate effort they will be successful. When dealing with pupils who frequently have learning difficulties and who may lack confidence and belief in themselves as learners, such help and expectations are of crucial importance. It is also important to convey that success lies in their own hands, and that they need to be aware of how they approach tasks, the degree of persistence they apply to be successful, and that there is no substitute for a willingness on their part to apply sustained effort.

Your relationships with pupils

A positive classroom climate very much depends on the type of relationship you establish with your pupils. Pupils' learning is most likely to flourish in a climate where this relationship is based on mutual respect and rapport between yourself and your pupils.

Mutual respect and rapport

Mutual respect largely develops from the pupils seeing by your actions that you are a competent teacher, and that you care about their progress by planning and conducting effective lessons and carrying out your various tasks with commitment. In addition, you convey in your dealings with pupils, both during whole class teaching and in your interactions with individuals, that you respect each pupil as an individual who has individual and personal needs.

Good rapport stems from conveying to pupils that you understand, share and value their perspective, as individuals, on a whole range of matters and experiences, academic, social and personal. For example, sympathizing that the local football team got knocked out of a cup competition, praise for a pupil who had performed well in a school play, concern that a pupil has a bad cold, and excitement that a school trip is near. The development of a positive classroom climate depends on this relationship being two-way: your respect for pupils should be reciprocated in their respect for you, and your understanding of their perspectives reciprocated in their understanding of your's. Nevertheless, as an adult, and given your role, it is up to you to have a major influence in establishing such a harmonious relationship in the classroom.

The skills involved in establishing a climate of mutual respect and rapport are highly prized in schools, as they also have a major impact on the general climate of the school as a whole. They also contribute to the pastoral care role of the teacher, and make it easier for pupils to come to you with their personal problems and difficulties. Indeed, a study by Grace (1984) noted that a high proportion of outstanding teachers in inner-city comprehensive schools were skilful in developing good rapport with potentially difficult and demanding adolescents, and that not surprisingly, many of these outstanding teachers had specific pastoral care responsibilities in the school as a result. Pye (1988) interestingly noticed how skilful teachers were able to convey a personal manner in interaction with an individual pupil during a private exchange, in which the mutual respect and rapport established was particularly evident. Pye described this as a situation in which the teacher and pupil were 'acknowledging' each other; *viz* they had established a personal relationship which was separate from, and yet still part of, the relationship that the teacher had with the class as a whole.

Acting as a good example

It is also important to be aware of the influence that your behaviour can have on pupils in acting as an example or model for their own behaviour. This identification with the teacher is particularly strong in the primary school years, but for most pupils is still very much in evidence in the secondary school years as well. Pupils will expect you to be a good example of the expectations that you convey. If you insist on neat work, your own blackboard work should also be neat. If you expect pupils to act in a civilised manner, you should not lose your temper or use sarcasm to hurt their feelings. If you want pupils to find the work interesting, you should convey interest in the activities yourself. Indeed, in reports based on their classroom observations, the HMI (eg HMI, 1987) have noted the particular importance of the example set by the teacher in establishing a positive ethos in the classroom.

The use of humour

One of the difficulties facing beginning teachers concerns knowing whether, how and when to use humour in the classroom, and the extent to which their relationship with pupils should be friendly. Judicious use of humour and conveying that you have a sense of humour can play a useful part in helping to establish good rapport and a positive classroom climate. Humour can be used to good effect in a whole range of situations, including introducing a light-hearted aspect of the work in hand or making a joke at your own expense (and, if done skilfully, making a joke at a pupil's expense but in a way that enables the pupil to share the joke rather than feel victimised). Humour can also be used to reassure a pupil who is anxious or in difficulties or to defuse a potential conflict with a pupil concerning misbehaviour. Conveying that you have a sense of humour is indicated in the way you respond to events that occur with good humour or share with pupils some amusement which they see in a situation. It might be something as simple as a remark you make when a piece of chalk you are writing with breaks, or how you react to pupil's aside (eg did a division of 'minute men' in the American War of Independence consist of three hours' worth?).

Linked with the use of humour is the extent to which you try to establish friendly relations with pupils. Part of establishing good rapport with pupils involves sharing to some extent each other's understanding and perspective of the demands of classroom life and life outside the classroom in general. This will include valuing and respecting each other as individuals and valuing each other's viewpoints. Much of this forms the basis of friendship between individuals. Nevertheless, the classroom is a unique, and, to a large extent, a very ritualised environment. To sustain order and control, your relationship with pupils, above all, must be one in which they respect and accept your authority to manage and control what happens in the classroom so that their learning may progress effectively. This means that your manner needs to be competent, business-like and task-oriented. Frequent use of humour, particularly being 'jokey', and trying to act as a friend of equal status, tends to undermine your authority because it does not accord with the ritual of school life and how pupils typically see and react to different aspects of a teacher's manner.

As a result, beginning teachers who attempt to build their relationships with pupils by frequent use of humour or an over-friendly approach, often find that they are less able to establish and exert their authority when required to do so. The ability to establish mutual respect and rapport in the classroom, and to use humour to good effect, and to be able to establish a friendly ethos without being too friendly, involves very sensitive social awareness on the teacher's part. It is somewhat like a chef who uses taste while cooking to decide on the right amount of salt to add to enhance the flavour of the dish rather than spoil it. Use of humour and friendship in the classroom can be seen as 'flavour enhancers' to add to the generally business-like and task-oriented manner you convey.

Enhancing pupils' self-esteem

Perhaps the single most important feature that has contributed to improving the quality of education provided in schools has been the increasing awareness amongst teachers of the importance of fostering pupils' self-esteem, self-confidence and self-respect as learners. Many writers have documented the ways in which schools can damage pupils' self-esteem by emphasizing for many pupils their relative lack of success compared with that of high-attaining pupils. As a result, such pupils attribute a sense of failure to the work they do, even if it is their best. In consequence, they may then get caught in a vicious downward spiral of under-achievement on their part and low expectations by teachers for their future work. Hargreaves (1982) refers to this process as involving the destruction of pupils' sense of dignity, in which they increasingly feel inferior, unable and powerless. He argues that this attack on their dignity stems not only from their experience of the 'formal curriculum', but also, and even more so, from their experience of the 'hidden curriculum'.

The formal curriculum refers to learning about the subject and topic being studied, whereas the hidden curriculum refers to all the messages conveyed to pupils by their experience of schools. These messages stem from the way they are treated, and the attitudes and values conveyed to them about their role and worth as individuals and the worth of what they have accomplished. Many of the messages conveyed in the hidden curriculum may be unintended. For example, if during classroom discussion with pupils you never use or elaborate on pupils' contributions, but always judge them simply in terms of whether they have contributed what you wanted in a narrowly conceived view of their correctness, pupils may get the message that their thoughts and ideas are of little worth or value except in so far as they are correct as judged by you. This may undermine the degree to which they are then willing to contribute ideas, particularly exploratory or uncertain ones which may be the opposite of what you would wish.

The humanistic approach to teaching and learning

The increasing awareness of the importance of fostering pupils' self-esteem has been a major development in recent years. This view of their importance has, however, a long pedigree, and stems in part from its emphasis within humanistic psychology and its applications to education, most notably through the work of Maslow and Rogers (eg Maslow, 1970; Rogers, 1983). They both argued that education must place an emphasis on the whole person, on the idea of personal growth, on the pupil's own perspective in terms of how they see themselves and see the world, and on the notion of personal agency and the power of choice. The key elements in applying such an approach to classroom teaching involves:

- seeing the teacher's role as essentially that of being a facilitator
- providing a significant degree of choice and control to pupils to manage and organise their own learning
- displaying respect for and empathy with pupils.

Fostering pupils' self-esteem is seen to lie at the heart of this approach. This perspective is evident, either explicitly or implicitly, in many important developments in classroom practice; in particular, the growth of active learning methods, as well as in the introduction of new forms of assessment, most notably that of records of achievement. Indeed, some lessons, such as those forming part of a personal and social education programme, eg the use of active tutorial work, may be designed to foster pupils' self-esteem in general as well as their self-esteem as learners in particular.

Conveying positive messages

The need to foster pupils' self-esteem as learners is fundamental to establishing a positive classroom climate, and the most important influence on pupils' self-esteem in the classroom is your interaction with the pupils. If your comments to pupils are largely positive, supportive, encouraging, praising, valuing and relaxing, rather than negative, depracating, harsh, attacking, dominating and anxiety-provoking, this will do much to foster pupils' self-esteem.

In addition, your body language also communicates to pupils how you feel about them, through messages conveyed non-verbally by your use of eye contact, posture, facial expression, and tone of voice. These can sometimes make it difficult to convey a message verbally about how you feel if your body language indicates to pupils something different. An awareness of how what you say and how your body language is likely to be perceived by pupils can help you to develop the skills involved in establishing a positive classroom climate. Nevertheless, positive messages are much easier to convey if you genuinely do feel in the ways you are trying to convey; *viz* you genuinely do like and respect pupils, care for their learning, and feel relaxed and confident in your role.

Giving positive help

In your interactions with pupils, the two areas that probably have the greatest effect concern how you treat pupils' errors and the extent to which you take a personal interest in their progress.

Pupil errors refer to any contribution, piece of work or learning difficulty which falls short of the standard of progress you desire. It includes a poor answer to a question, a poorly written-up project, or simply not being able to undertake a task you have set. In such circumstances you need to consider the type of feedback to give that will be helpful and supportive rather than admonishing. It is generally better to give specific help that relates to the task rather than critical feedback about performance or critical comments about the pupil. For example, pointing out that the pupil needs to remember that the hypotenuse is always the side opposite to the right angle, is better than simply saying 'You can do better than this' or, even worse, 'This is the low standard of work I have come to expect from you'. Also, when a pupil is having difficulties, you need to avoid sounding patronising. This can be difficult, because you are in authority and may, from time to time, be giving advice or diagnosing a difficulty that the pupil is already aware of. This should not be a problem, since the pupil should be willing to tolerate this if it only happens occasionally. The real problem arises if your tone is perceived by the pupil to be conveying an element of 'put down', sarcasm or unfair criticism. Thus, for example, telling a pupil whose diagram would have been much better if a sharpened pencil had been used that 'You should use a pencil sharpener because they're handy for sharpening pencils' would be considered unnecessarily hostile.

Taking a personal interest in each pupil's progress can be conveyed by relating what you say to each pupil and how you respond to their progress to their particular needs and previous work. Learning and using pupils' names with a new class as soon as possible is well worth-while, and you should certainly know their names after the first few weeks. During personal interactions, indicating to pupils how they are making progress and linking your comments to previous interactions does much to convey to each pupil that you are taking a personal interest in them as individuals, and, so far as possible, tailoring matters to meet their individual needs.

Classroom appearance and composition

There are two important features of a lesson that have a major influence on the classroom climate that develops, although neither is part of the lesson itself. The first concerns the general appearance of the classroom, including its layout and even the appearance of the teacher and that of the pupils. The second concerns the composition of the class, whether setted, mixed ability or mixed age in composition. Both these features convey strong messages through the hidden curriculum referred to earlier.

Classroom appearance
The general appearance of a classroom indicates to pupils the care that goes into providing them with an environment which is conducive to learning. A clean and well-kept room, with appropriate resources in evidence, which appears comfortable, light and well-aired, helps to establish a positive expectation towards the lesson. A positive mental set is also provided by appropriate use of posters and other visual displays concerning the type of work done in the classroom. Displays of pupils' work also indicate a pride in the work achieved, as well as acting as a motivator for those producing display work. Everywhere a pupil looks should convey positive expectations. The degree of light, space and air in the classrooms of many schools built since the 1950s has been generally very good. The use of temporary huts that have fallen into disrepair, however, has been very bad.

While the ethos in the classroom will, in part, be influenced by that of the school in general, each teacher can do much to improve the appearance of their own room, should you, as most teachers do, have your own room. For subject specialists in secondary schools, your room should act as an invitation to the subject. For example, entering a foreign language classroom should immerse pupils into signals of the foreign countries, most notably through use of posters, maps and even objects from those countries. While primary school classrooms will be host to a variety of activities, it is often possible to create areas which are subject specific, and which can also act as resource areas or as focal points for particular activities.

Layout

The layout of the room should be functional for the purposes intended. At the very least, you and the blackboard should be clearly visible. There is much debate concerning the importance of using a layout to match the general style of teaching and learning which takes place. In 'open classrooms', characterised by more active learning methods, including frequent use of group work, movement of pupils between areas, the use of resource centres, independent work using workcards or computer packages, the seating arrangements will almost certainly require desks to be grouped together and the use of activity specific areas. In 'traditional classrooms', which emphasize didactic teaching, formal rows of desks are more appropriate. Unfortunately, the large size of some classes in relation to the size of the room, often places severe constraints on teachers in some schools in creating the most functionally efficient layout. Fortunately, many modern primary schools were designed with open classrooms in mind. This has allowed functionally efficient layouts to be developed, some even making use of movable walls. Secondary schools have generally been much less flexible in this respect. Some schools have developed resource centres housed in rooms of their own, where teachers can send a pupil or groups of pupils to undertake particular tasks, either unsupervised or supervised by a teacher based in the resource centre.

Tidiness

It is also very important to keep the classroom clean and tidy. This can have a marked impact on pupils when they first arrive at the classroom, whether it be at the beginning of the school day or after a break. In primary schools one can make efforts to ensure that pupils themselves help to keep things tidy and avoid making a mess. This tends to be more difficult in secondary schools, where you will be teaching many different classes, and may not always be using your own room. If on occasions you take over a room where desks and tables have been left disarranged, it is well worthwhile to tidy up quickly before your class arrives. You, of course, also have a responsibility to colleagues to ensure that any room you leave is fit and ready for the next user, which includes cleaning the blackboard. This is all part of having a professional attitude towards your work.

Dress

Your appearance conveys messages to pupils about the care and attention you give to presentation in general. It is the case that in our society, dress conveys signals about status and about your formal role. However, the norms which operate here are changing all the time. For example, in some schools, school uniform is worn by pupils, female teachers are expected not to wear trousers, most male teachers wear a jacket and tie, teachers may be addressed as 'Sir' or 'Miss' and pupils by their surnames. At the other extreme, there are schools where none of these apply. Whatever else, you will need to adapt to the conventions and expectations that operate in your school, as radical deviations away from these are likely to be misunderstood by pupils, although some degree of departure in the direction you feel is educationally worthwhile is acceptable and desirable. Nevertheless, your behaviour in the classroom must take account of your role in also contributing to a consistent and coherent attempt by staff in the school as a whole to operate as a team in developing and emphasizing certain values and expectations.

While you will have little control over pupils' dress, other than dealing with major departures from school conventions (such as wearing ear-rings or jeans), it is important to insist they arrive at the lesson prepared for the tasks to be undertaken, with appropriate equipment, pens, pencils, rulers, etc. Bags should not be left on desks and coats should not be worn. In some schools such apparently minor matters can

Your appearance will convey a message about you

involve a lot of time and effort by teachers to deal with. In such cases, well-developed routines are of immense value in helping to ensure that a prompt start to the lesson is not delayed.

Class composition
The composition of the class also conveys important messages. A class composed of pupils setted or streamed in terms of attainment will almost certainly have an influence on pupils' expectations about themselves and on your expectations about them. It is particularly important to ensure that those groups identified as average or below average in attainment are neither discouraged by this nor under-achieve as a result.

Mixed-ability groups are often used to convey a sense of equal valuing of all pupils, which in part explains their widespread adoption in comprehensive schools and in primary schools, although in the latter it is often simply the most convenient form of group given the size of the year group. In some primary schools, cross-age groups are used, and in particularly small schools, a class may be composed of quite a wide age range. Other aspects of pupil composition of importance include social class mix, ethnic origin mix, and the proportion of able pupils or pupils with learning difficulties. All such factors have an important bearing on teaching and learning. They also have an important bearing on the type of classroom climate that develops, and on the ways you can best facilitate a positive classroom climate. The key factor here is the skill involved in developing mutual respect and rapport that takes the composition of the class into account. Establishing your authority, being sociable and motivating pupils will require different shared understandings and points of reference with some classes composed in certain of these respects, compared with classes composed very differently.

Thus, for example, the way in which pupils in general may react to your use of humour, how supportive your feedback is, the way you exert discipline and how you try to personalise interactions, may well be quite different for a group of racially-mixed pupils in an infant class in a school serving a relatively deprived urban catchment, compared with a group of top-set pupils in a mathematics lesson in a comprehensive school serving a prosperous rural catchment. An important aspect of your skill in establishing a positive classroom climate involves your sensitivity to the effect of your behaviour on the type of pupils that make up the class and the context within which this occurs.

Key questions about your classroom climate

1 *Is the classroom climate purposeful, task-oriented, relaxed, warm, supportive and does it have a sense of order?*

2 *Do my comments, particularly feedback on their progress, help pupils to develop self-esteem and self-respect as learners?*

3 *Are the learning activities challenging and do they offer realistic opportunities for success?*

4 *Do I make good use of both intrinsic and extrinsic sources of pupil motivation?*

5 *Does my behaviour convey positive expectations?*

6 *Do I successfully convey a personal interest and care for the progress of each pupil?*

7 *Is my relationship with pupils based on mutual respect and rapport?*

8 *Do the messages conveyed by the nature and types of activities used and the way I interact with pupils contribute to establishing a positive classroom climate?*

9 *Does the appearance and layout of the classroom convey positive expectations and facilitate the activities which occur?*

10 *Do I take adequate account of the influence of the composition of the class (eg spread of ability, social class mix) on the way I can best establish a positive classroom climate?*

6 Discipline

Discipline refers to the order which is necessary in the classroom for pupil learning to occur effectively. There is a massive amount of literature on discipline in schools, which includes a number of books offering sound practical advice (eg Johnstone and Munn, 1987; Kyriacou, 1986a; Robertson, 1989; Rogers, 1989), and a major government report on the topic: the Elton Report (DES, 1989a). Discipline is one of the major areas of concern for student teachers, and is also identified in the Elton Report as a major area of need within the in-service education of experienced teachers.

Clearly, order is needed in the classroom if the activities which take place are to facilitate effective learning by pupils. The most important point to bear in mind in considering discipline, is that creating the necessary order is more to do with the skills involved in effective teaching in general than it is to do with how you deal with pupil misbehaviour itself. If the learning activities are well-planned and prepared, if the presentation elicits and maintains pupils' attention, interest and involvement, and if the activities are challenging and offer realistic opportunities for success, then the necessary order will be established as part of these qualities. In essence, skilful teaching as outlined in the previous chapters lies at the heart of establishing discipline. Nevertheless, pupil misbehaviour will occur from time to time, even in the lessons of the most skilful teachers, and has to be dealt with. However, it is a mistake to view discipline as something concerned with how you deal with pupil misbehaviour, separate from your general teaching. It is an even worse mistake to try to establish discipline by focusing on how to dominate and engender fear in pupils as a strategy for minimising misbehaviour. Such a course of action is undesirable, not only because it will undermine you creating the positive classroom climate necessary to facilitate pupils learning effectively, but also because it directs your attention away from considering how to develop the quality of your teaching as the primary means of establishing order.

The nature of pupil misbehaviour

Most pupil misbehaviour is quite trivial. The types of pupil misbehaviour most frequently cited by teachers are:

- excessive talk or talking out of turn
- being noisy (both verbal, such as shouting to another pupil across the room, and non-verbal, such as letting a desk lid slam shut)
- not paying attention to the teacher
- not getting on with the work required
- being out of their seat without good cause
- hindering other pupils
- arriving late for lessons.

(eg DES, 1989a; Wragg and Dooley, 1984). To a large extent, such problems can be minimised by skilful teaching in general, and by developing conventions and routines for behaviour which are followed. More serious types of misbehaviour (verbal aggression to another pupil, bad language and cheek, disobedience, refusal to accept authority, and physical destructiveness) are much less frequent and are likely to occur if the lesser forms of pupil misbehaviour are allowed to become commonplace, or if pupils are reacting against personal and academic difficulties they are facing.

In thinking about pupil misbehaviour, we need to remember that there is a continuum of such behaviour ranging from quite trivial acts to very serious ones. Moreover, the standard of behaviour expected will vary from teacher to teacher. One teacher may insist on virtual silence in a lesson while pupils are working, whereas another might be happy with a marked degree of background talking. In addition, pupils will also vary in their attitudes towards good behaviour. Some pupils will be happy to wait quietly while a teacher looks for some equipment in a storeroom, whereas some pupils will be poised to take any such opportunity to engage in rowdy behaviour. The discipline which prevails in your classroom will not only be influenced by your behaviour and expectations, but also by the expectations pupils bring with them, and, importantly, by the prevailing ethos in the school. Nevertheless, a well-managed lesson coupled with a relationship based on mutual respect and rapport will do much to minimise pupil misbehaviour. Indeed, even in schools where it is recognised that there are a number of pupils with marked emotional or academic difficulties, skilful teaching can ensure that good discipline in lessons will be the norm.

Causes of pupil misbehaviour
In general, you can start with the assumption that all pupils will be willing to engage in the work, and are only likely to misbehave if there are specific reasons or motives for doing so. As such, your task is to make it as easy as possible for pupils to sustain good behaviour. The main causes of misbehaviour in the classroom are as follows.

Boredom. If the activities are presented in a manner that fails to elicit and sustain their interest, or if the activity lasts for too long and fails to be stimulating, or if the activity is too easy or is felt to lack relevance, then pupils are likely to become bored.

Prolonged mental effort. Most academic work requires sustained mental effort, and this is demanding. Everyone finds that sustaining mental effort for long periods is difficult and, at times, unpleasant.

Inability to do the work. Pupils may be unable to do the work set, either because it is too difficult or because they are unclear about the task demands.

Being sociable. Pupils have a complex social life in schools, in which friendships are made, conflicts arise and interests are shared. Aspects of these social relationships between pupils will often spill over into a lesson (eg pupils may resume a conversation started during the break period).

Low academic self-esteem. Some pupils will lack confidence in themselves as learners, and may have experienced frequent failure in the past that makes them reluctant to engage in further tasks for fear of further failure (failing because you did not try is much less painful than failing if you did). Such pupils can become quite alienated from the academic expectations which form part of a positive classroom climate.

Emotional difficulties. Some pupils may have emotional problems which make it difficult for them to adjust to and cope with the demands of school life and the academic demands of the classroom. It may be because they are being bullied in school, or because they are neglected at home. In many cases, such pupils may become attention-seeking, and actually enjoy the attention they provoke from you or their fellow pupils for misbehaving.

Poor attitudes. Some pupils may simply not value doing well at school, and to the extent that problems arise, such as finding the work boring or difficult, will switch off their effort. Moreover, some may try to avoid doing the work by arriving late to lessons, or keeping a low profile while doing little. When challenged, they may be apologetic or hostile, but still do little. Some pupils may deliberately make a nuisance of themselves simply to cause excitement.

Lack of negative consequences. Whenever a pupil misbehaves, your actions that follow in consequence must be aimed at getting the pupil involved in the work again as quickly as possible. Furthermore, your behaviour should act to dissuade such pupil misbehaviour occurring again in similar circumstances. If pupil misbehaviour is not picked up quickly and discouraged by the consequences that follow, it is likely to become more frequent.

Implications for teaching

It will be evident from looking at these main causes of pupil misbehaviour that they have different implications for how you can best deal with such incidents. For example, if a pupil fails to pay attention because they are finding the topic boring, your best course of action will be quite different than if the problem stems from worries and anxieties the pupil has because the work seems too difficult. Part of the skill of teaching involves being sensitive to the different causes of pupil misbehaviour. While most of the time sound management techniques and the most obvious assumption about the cause of the misbehaviour are appropriate, skilful teachers are alert to circumstances where an exploratory probe in private is needed. This will be evident if a pupil's behaviour appears to be out of character or if the normal management techniques do not appear to be having their expected effect. Skilful teachers are also very adept at picking up subtle cues from a pupil's facial expression or tone of voice that might indicate an underlying cause for concern.

An important point to bear in mind about the causes of misbehaviour is that pupils are a captive audience. Unlike many activities in life, where we have some degree of choice over whether we participate and can often withdraw from a situation which we find unpleasant, pupils are required to attend lessons. Moreover, they are not allowed to opt out of learning. As such, all teaching has an implicit tension underlying the activities that if pupils do not engage freely in the activities set up by the teacher, they will be coerced to do so. Poor progress is not simply the concern of the pupil, but also the concern of the teacher and the pupil's parents. Most people will find, from time to time, that being trapped in a situation that is unpleasant and from which they cannot escape extremely frustrating. If coercion to participate is also exerted, the sense of frustration can become unbearable. The most serious incidents of pupil misbehaviour are likely to occur when such a tension has built up, and when the pupil feels your attention is aggresive coercion rather than sympathetic and supportive. A warning signal of this might be the pupil looking increasingly angry or tense, and perhaps claiming to be picked upon or treated unfairly in some way. The skills involved in being sensitive to whether a pupil is feeling tense in this way, and the ability to defuse such a feeling, is very important in preventing serious incidents occurring.

Establishing your authority

The key to establishing good discipline in the classroom lies in pupils accepting your authority to manage their behaviour and their progress in learning. Learning activities cannot take place effectively in a classroom full of 30 pupils unless you are given authority to control, manage and direct what is going on as, when and how appropriate. All pupils recognise this from their earliest days in school, but it is important to note that this authority is given to you to act as a manager of their learning rather than as a power relationship. A useful analogy is with the authority you give to a tour guide to show you around places of interest in a particular city. You obey instructions concerning where and when to go to different places and what to do there because you trust and expect that in doing so you will get to see what is worth seeing efficiently. Your trust largely rests on the expertise and skill you expect your tour guide to have. Similarly, establishing your authority as a teacher largely depends on four main aspects of your role:

- conveying your status
- teaching competently
- exercising managerial control
- dealing with pupil misbehaviour effectively.

Conveying your status

Much of your authority as a teacher derives from the status you have in that role, and the respect and esteem for teachers generally held in society; this is particularly conveyed to pupils by their parents and other sources of influence. You are also an adult, and will have some degree of status because of this, most notably with younger pupils where you may be perceived as a parent figure to some extent. If you have a post of seniority in the school, such as being the headteacher or head of department, then this will also add to your status.

The most important thing about status, however, is not that you simply have such status, but that you act as though you have status. This conveys to pupils a sense of you being in charge and in authority that they simply take for granted. Behaving as though you have status will be conveyed by your appearing relaxed, self-assured and confident, as indicated in particular by your tone of voice, posture, facial expression and use of eye contact. When you issue an instruction, your tone will indicate by its matter-of-factness that you simply expect without question that the instruction will be followed.

Status is also conveyed by various actions that indicate you have status. Most notably, the fact that you are free to wander around the

Conveying your status

classroom, initiate conversations and direct activities. You also take the decisions about when pupils are to start and stop particular activities. Again, it is by acting in these ways in a manner that indicates that you are in charge that you create a climate in which your authority is taken for granted. This requires that as well as behaving in these ways yourself, you control such behaviour by pupils; *viz* pupils cannot wander about, decide when to stop activities, or when to initiate conversations with you or with each other unless it is with your permission and appropriate. Thus, for example, most teachers will make a point of picking up on pupils who have started to pack away their books near the end of a lesson before they have been told to do so.

It is perhaps worth noting that one aspect of conveying status you need to be careful about is the use of touch. It is quite common for those in a position of higher status to touch those of lower status, in a friendly and caring manner, but not vice versa. However, you do need to be aware that in the classroom, touching pupils in this way can be misunderstood and, in part depending on the pupil's personal circumstances, even undesirable or unpleasant. While many teachers can use touch successfully as part of conveying warmth, you do need to be alert to possible problems that can can arise, and it is often safest to avoid using touch unless you are absolutely sure of the consequences of doing so.

Teaching competently

The second major source of your authority comes from teaching competently. If you convey to pupils that you are knowledgeable about the topic or subject, are interested in it, and can set up the learning activities skilfully, then pupils will respect your ability to teach; this will confirm your authority to manage their behaviour. This requires that your lessons are well-planned and prepared, that your manner conveys interest and enthusiasm, and that you can set up challenging activities effectively.

One of the reasons that teaching competently is so crucial to establishing your authority, is because poor teaching is often experienced as insulting. When pupils are taught in a way they regard as unsatisfactory, then one of two interpretations are commonly drawn by pupils. Either that the teacher has not made an effort which implies that the pupils are not worth making an effort for, or that the school has allocated them a teacher who lacks adequate teaching skills which implies that the pupils were not worth being allocated a better teacher. Both interpretations strike at the heart of pupils' self-esteem, and the extent that they may react by misbehaviour is largely related to the underlying insult they experience. In contrast, being taught competently engenders a feeling of pride and self-respect, and affirms their sense of worth and importance.

Exercising managerial control

The third major source of your authority comes from exercising managerial control in the classroom. In order to set up learning activities efficiently, lessons need to get off to a prompt start, pupils must be kept involved in the learning activities, and transitions between activities should be handled smoothly. Anything that frustrates these will require you to exert managerial control. Pupils arriving late for lessons, not paying attention or applying sufficient effort, or interrupting your presentation, can frustrate the prompt start and flow of the lesson. Laslett and Smith (1984) identified the four main tasks of classroom management as 'Get them in, get them out, get on with it, and get on with them'!

The most crucial aspects of exercising managerial control involve establishing clear conventions, routines and expectations for pupils' behaviour, and imposing your view on a situation when any conflicts arise. For example, if when you are ready to start the lesson a pupil points out that they need a new exercise book, then rather than allow the start of the lesson to be delayed, particularly if you have called pupils to attention, you should indicate you will deal with that later and proceed promptly with the lesson. Once the lesson is in progress virtually any activity can frustrate the progress of the lesson. For example, giving out equipment can take too long or become cumbersome, the pace of work by pupils may be rather slow, or pupils may take a long time to pay attention to you after an activity has been completed. To prevent progress being frustrated, you need to exercise your control whenever appropriate.

In order to exercise managerial control, pupils' behaviour needs to be rule-governed. Such classroom rules may be explicitly stated by teachers or simply inferred from the teacher's actions. Wragg and Wood (1984) identified the following rules as being the most common ones recorded in their study based on classroom observations:

- no talking when teacher is talking (public situation)
- no disruptive noises
- rules for entering, leaving and moving about in the classroom
- no interference with the work of others
- work must be completed in a specified way
- pupils must raise hand to answer and not shout out
- pupils must make a positive effort in their work
- pupils must not challenge the authority of the teacher
- respect must be shown for property and equipment
- rules to do with safety
- pupils must ask if they do not understand.

Unpredictable events, such as the appearance of a window cleaner, can be disruptive, although a quick acknowledgement of the situation with a touch of humour is often effective in such circumstances. Imposing your will simply means ensuring that pupils do what you want them to do to ensure that the lesson progresses.

Dealing with pupil misbehaviour effectively

From time to time, pupil misbehaviour will occur. This may range from a trivial incident, such as a pupil not paying attention, to a serious one, such as a pupil punching another in anger. How you deal with pupil behaviour is the fourth major source of your authority. Your authority will be enhanced to the extent that you are able to deal with pupil misbehaviour effectively and fairly. How to do this is the subject of the remainder of this chapter.

Pre-empting pupil misbehaviour

In considering pupil misbehaviour 'prevention is better than cure'. Skilful teaching can do much to minimise pupil misbehaviour occurring in the first place, and can usefully re-direct incidents that were developing before they need be regarded as misbehaviour. The essence of pre-empting misbehaviour lies in vigilance plus action.

Strategies to pre-empt misbehaviour

Careful monitoring of pupils' behaviour and progress during a lesson can ensure that most misbehaviour is nipped in the bud. Successful monitoring requires a conscious decision to do so periodically, as it is all too easy to get wrapped up in particular activities, such as giving individual help, and thereby not to notice another pupil who is disrupting someone else's work. Experienced teachers are adept at such monitoring, while student teachers can usefully remind themselves to do this until it becomes routine.

The main useful strategies to pre-empt misbehaviour are as follows.

Scan the classroom.   Periodically look around the classroom and consider whether any pupils appear to be having difficulties and, if so, go over and investigate in a supportive and helpful manner to ensure that pupils resume working as quickly as possible. Individual contact will be more effective than shouting across the room. The latter both disrupts other pupils unnecessarily and tends to assume the pupil is misbehaving.

Circulate.   Circulate around the room periodically and probe whether pupils are having difficulties. Sometimes asking a pupil about their progress usefully uncovers problems which they would otherwise not have drawn to your attention.

Make eye contact.   When addressing the class as a whole, make eye contact with individual pupils periodically, but do not look too long at any individual. If you suspect a pupil may be misbehaving, making eye contact, and prolonging it, will indicate to that pupil your awareness of their need to re-involve themselves in the lesson without needing to signal this publicly or interrupt the flow of the lesson.

Target your questions.   Directing your questions around the class helps to maintain pupils' involvement; targeting questions at particular individuals is also a signal to them to get re-involved.

Use proximity.   While you normally stand at the front of the classroom, how and where you move to can be an effective signal of your monitoring. By moving towards two pupils talking, you can indicate your awareness to them of this without interrupting the lesson. You may also stand near a pair or group of pupils for some time to sustain their working.

Give academic help.   Giving advice and guidance to pupils to enable and encourage them to make progress with the task in hand is the single most powerful means of pre-empting misbehaviour.

Change activities or pace.   As a result of monitoring pupils' progress you may feel the lesson is proceeding too slowly or too fast and that pupils are ready to move on to another activity or are running into difficulties. Your decisions about altering the pace of the lesson and when to change the activity are crucial to maintaining pupils' involvement. This applies not only to the class as a whole, but also to individual pupils, some of whom will often need to work at a different pace or on a diferent activity, even when whole class teaching is taking place, if they are to sustain their involvement to best effect.

Notice misbehaviour.   If a pupil is misbehaving, in the vast majority of cases it is important to indicate to the pupil that you have noticed this. Eye contact may be sufficient, or if you wish to do this more forcefully, a stern facial expression or a pause in your exposition will indicate your concern and displeasure, while not interrupting the flow of the lesson for more than a moment. Student teachers often tend to refrain from doing this, in part because they feel misbehaviour needs to be more formally reprimanded once it is noticed or because they hope it might disappear if ignored. In fact, signalling of this sort is very important and effective in exercising managerial control; failing to do so by ignoring simply allows more frequent or serious misbehaviour to develop, whereas too ready a recourse to reprimands serves to create a conflict unnecessarily.

Notice disrespect.   When interacting with pupils you should expect pupils to behave with appropriate respect. Thus, for example, if a pupil is slouched in their seat when addressed by you, it would be a normal courtesy for the pupil to quickly sit up straight while replying. Not doing so might be dealt with by your looking surprised or stern to indicate you are not happy with this, and if that is not sufficient, you might comment explicitly. Lack of courtesy or respect towards you needs to be picked up as it forms part of pupils' impressions concerning the standard of behaviour you expect and the type of relationship you wish to establish. Not doing so will tacitly undermine your authority in behaving with status and exercising managerial control on your terms.

Move pupils.   If the circumstances warrant, do not hesitate to separate two pupils who are not behaving acceptably together, after due warning to this effect. Alternatively, you may require a particular pupil to sit at the front where you can monitor the pupil's behaviour more closely. Seating arrangements are a privilege rather than a right of pupils, and if you feel a better arrangement is desirable, a move can be helpful. However, you need to emphasize that this is done in the pupils' interests to ensure that any resentment is minimised.

Sound discipline largely rests on skilful teaching and skilful use of such strategies to pre-empt misbehaviour. Even so, misbehaviour will still occur from time to time, and to deal with this, the best strategy is to combine the use of investigating and counselling with the use of reprimands.

Investigating and counselling

When pupil misbehaviour has occurred despite your use of pre-emptive strategies, you have a choice to make between investigating the nature and cause of the misbehaviour or reprimanding the misbehaviour on the basis of your reading of its most likely nature and cause. Your decision will very much depend on the context, such as the pupil concerned, the nature of the activities taking place, how certain you are about your reading of the incident, and what you anticipate will be the most likely effect of any action you take.

Investigating and counselling refers to a strategy whereby you approach the incident of misbehaviour with a view to finding out the nature of the problem. Indeed, your comment to the pupil might well be 'What's the problem?'. Your tone should indicate your concern with a view to helping the pupil return to the work in hand as soon as possible, rather than convey hostility or aggression on your part. In such circumstances, the pupil may admit to having problems with the work, or may attribute the misbehaviour to being bored, being pro- voked by another pupil, or whatever. If the nature of the problem is not primarily an academic difficulty, you then need to decide whether to counsel the pupil towards behaving appropriately there and then or else seeing the pupil at the end of the lesson, during a break time or after school.

Effective counselling

When counselling a pupil it is important to allow the pupil to do much of the talking, with a view to helping the pupil see that the mis- behaviour is not in their interests, and that the pupil should agree to behave as required in future. Such counselling is likely to be more effective if conducted in private, in a context of trust and mutual respect, and where you convey a caring and concerned attitude. It is important to get the pupil to evaluate his/her own behaviour and to consider the consequences, such as poor academic progress or punish- ments, that may follow if the behaviour does not improve. The most important aspect of counselling is to end with the pupil agreeing to behave well in future as a positive decision.

Where such counselling does not appear to be successful or serious problems appear to be underlying the misbehaviour, it is important to confer with colleagues who have explicit pastoral care concerns. In secondary schools, this will be the form teacher and the head of house or year, although in many schools it is usual for the head of department to be involved in the first instance. In primary schools, the class teacher is normally the form teacher as well, and thus consultation is likely to involve the headteacher or a deputy head with specific responsibility for pastoral care.

Your pastoral care role
In your role as a class teacher, you must bear in mind that you simultaneously have a pastoral care role. Hence, as well as being concerned about pupils' academic progress, you must also be concerned about their general behaviour and attitudes, their personal and social development, and any individual needs they may have. Dealing with pupil misbehaviour is not simply a matter of discipline, but is also bound up with your pastoral care responsibilities.

In addition, in this respect, you should also be alert to pupils' behaviour giving cause for concern that may not undermine discipline or be regarded as misbehaviour. For example, excessive shyness, a tendency to work very slowly, or frequent day-dreaming, may not be in any way disruptive, but may well need to be picked up in monitoring pupils' progress and may well need to be investigated further. A study I was involved in looked at teachers' views about pupils' behaviour problems in a comprehensive school, and noted that while teachers cited a number of disruptive behaviours as serious or undesirable behaviour problems, they also cited some non-disruptive behaviours (Kyriacou and Roe, 1988).

Resulting actions
As a result of investigating and counselling by you alone or in wider consultation with colleagues, there may well be actions you need to take to assist the pupil to behave well. For example, you may discover that the pupil finds it difficult to settle down to work because they are easily distracted by certain other pupils, or the pupil is finding the work too difficult or is getting late nights at home. Some pupils may have a special educational need that requires a formal assessment to be made and explicit provision, such as the help of a support teacher for a period (see Hanko, 1985). Some of the necessary actions can be taken by you in the classroom, others may involve collaboration with colleagues, particularly if parents and other agencies need to be involved.

Using reprimands

A reprimand refers to an explicit verbal warning or comment by you to a pupil which indicates your disapproval of the misbehaviour which has occurred. Because the use of investigating and counselling is time-consuming and logistically too difficult to be used for every misbehaviour which occurs, most misbehaviour that has not been successfully dealt with by the pre-emptive strategies will be dealt with by reprimands; only a minority of problems are dealt with by recourse to investigating and counselling. However, the balance between these two strategies will vary greatly from lesson to lesson and from class to class.

Effective use of reprimands

Reprimands are best used sparingly and should complement skilful teaching in general. Too frequent a use of reprimands will lessen their effect, will undermine creating a positive classroom climate, and is experienced by some pupils as 'nagging'.

A number of qualities are involved in the skilful and effective use of reprimands.

Correct targeting. The pupil being reprimanded should be correctly identified as the pupil instigating or engaged in the misbehaviour. A particular danger here is to reprimand a pupil who was reacting to another's provocation.

Firmness. Your reprimand should be clear and firm in tone and content. Avoid pleading or implying damage limitation (eg 'Let's at least get some decent work done in the last ten minutes') or softening your reprimand once issued.

Express concern. Your reprimand should convey your concern with the pupil's interests or that of other pupils being harmed by the misbehaviour.

Avoid anger. While a firm expression of disapproval is effective, expressing intense anger, shouting at pupils, and appearing to have lost your temper will tend to undermine a positive classroom climate. Frequent expressions of anger are undesirable, are experienced by pupils as unpleasant, and with younger pupils in particular, may be very upsetting.

Emphasize what is required. Reprimands should emphasize what pupils should be doing rather than simply complain about the misbehaviour itself. 'Pay attention' is better than 'Stop looking out of the window' and 'You may talk quietly with your neighbour' is better than 'There's too much noise in here'.

Maintain psychological impact. When a reprimand is given, its impact is enhanced by non-verbal cues, such as eye contact. After the reprimand is given, a momentary prolonging of eye contact together with a slight pause before continuing with the lesson can increase the force of the exchange.

Avoid confrontations.   Do not force a pupil into a heated exchange. Where such a possibility seems likely because the pupil appears tense, agitated or unresponsive to your pre-emptive strategies, postponing a reprimand and instead using investigating and counselling strategies would be appropriate. If you reprimand a pupil who then reacts emotionally, you can usefully curtail the exchange by telling the pupil to stay behind at the end of the lesson in a matter of fact manner and quickly resume the lesson.

Criticize the behaviour not the pupil.   It is important to emphasize that you disapprove of the misbehaviour not the pupil. This enables you to convey a sense of caring for the pupil and their interests, and gives pupils an opportunity to dissociate themselves from such misbehaviour in future. 'You need to concentrate more on your work and spend less time chatting to others' is better than 'You're an idle pupil'.

Use private rather than public reprimands.   A private reprimand, such as a quiet word, is useful because it is a more personal contact and lessens the likelihood of embarrassing the pupil and the chance that the pupil might react with hostility. It is also less disruptive on other pupils. A public reprimand to a pupil is better only when there is a specific reason to go public, such as when you actually want the whole class to hear the reprimand as an implicit warning to others. A less disruptive use of a public reprimand is to simply call out the pupil's name in a tone that conveys that you have noticed some misbehaviour which must stop immediately.

Pre-emptive.   Reprimands aimed at pre-empting misbehaviour are more effective than those which follow only after repeated and prolonged misbehaviour.

State rules and rationale.   A reprimand can usefully consist of a statement of the rule being transgressed together with an explanation of why the rule is required for the benefit of teaching and learning (eg 'Please put up your hand and wait until I ask you to speak so that everyone gets a fair chance to contribute and we can all hear what is said').

Avoid making hostile remarks.   Hostile and deprecating remarks should be avoided, as pupils may feel personally disliked, and may become disaffected and alienated. Sarcasm and ridicule in particular are felt by pupils to be unfair, and can undermine mutual respect and rapport to the detriment of a positive classroom climate.

Avoid unfair comparisons. Pupils tend to feel reprimands which involve stereotyping or comparisons with others are unfair, particularly if they relate to other members of the pupil's family or other classes (eg 'Your sister's work was much better than this' or 'Just because this is set three doesn't mean you don't have to pay attention').

Be consistent. Reprimands should relate to clear and consistently applied expectations. Pupils will resent being reprimanded if they feel the behaviour was not the type you would normally reprimand or if the severity of the reprimand was unexpectedly great.

Do not make empty threats. Do not issue reprimands that threaten consequences you would not wish to or could not carry out (eg 'The next pupil who talks will go straight to the head' or 'If you make another insolent remark, I shall be contacting your parents'). If you explicitly state consequences that will follow, it is very important to carry these out if you are to maintain credibility when you use this strategy in future.

Avoid reprimanding the whole class. Reprimanding the whole class is a serious act and should only be used when certain misbehaviour or your cause for concern is so widespread that individual reprimands will not have sufficient effect or be appropriate. In order to avoid casting your criticism equally on all pupils, including the blameless, it is useful to indicate your concern with 'too many pupils' rather than all pupils. A useful alternative is to discuss with the class as a whole why certain misbehaviour has become widespread, so that you can identify any particular problems and reinforce the need for good behaviour.

Make an example. Another useful alternative to reprimanding the whole class is to issue a particularly forceful reprimand to one pupil, and add or imply that you will not tolerate other pupils acting in this way. Reprimanding an individual can have just as much impact on the behaviour of the class as reprimanding the whole class. Making an example can be particularly useful in the first few lessons with a new class to highlight your expectations, such as how you deal with the first pupil who arrives late for your lessons without any excuse. It is also useful if certain pupils appear to be trying to challenge your authority publicly; however, you must be sensitive concerning whether you are simply being drawn into a public confrontation that is best dealt with in some other way.

Ideally the use of reprimands can be thought of as adding a few drops of oil to an engine that is running well but very occasionally needs further lubrication to maintain its smooth operation. Once the use of reprimands becomes frequent, the climate of the lesson can change quite markedly, and the tone becomes one of the teacher trying to coerce and cajole pupils towards working well. In such circumstances you need to think carefully whether the academic demands made upon pupils can be improved and consider the nature of the underlying causes of such continuing conflict.

Indeed, frequent misbehaviour by pupils acts as an on-going critique by pupils of the demands made upon them, and has acted as a major stimulus for curriculum development. The point being stressed here is that if the skilful use of reprimands does not appear to be successful, you should not assume that the best way ahead is to resort to more frequent and more severe reprimands and the use of punishments or other related strategies without also thinking long and hard about the educational context within which the problem over discipline as arisen.

Using punishments

Despite the skilful use of reprimands and other strategies already discussed, pupil misbehaviour may persist. In such circumstances, the use of punishments may be effective in restoring discipline.

The nature and purpose of punishment

A punishment is in essence a formal action which the pupil is intended to experience as unpleasant as a means of helping the pupil to behave appropriately in future. The dividing line between a reprimand and a punishment is often blurred because reprimands and other strategies are often also experienced as unpleasant. The difference largely lies in the formal way in which a punishment is set up and the explicit intention for it to be unpleasant.

In setting up a punishment, you thus need to emphasize to the pupil that the use of punishment is intended to help the pupil appreciate the gravity and seriousness with which you are treating the misbehaviour and the urgency of the need for acceptable behaviour to occur in future. Indeed, it is essential that the pupil sees the punishment as being in their own interests, and certainly not as an expression of malice or hostility.

Punishments have three main purposes:

- *retribution*: the idea that justice requires that wrongdoing is followed by a morally deserved punishment

- *deterrence*: the idea that the pupil or other pupils will wish to avoid such misbehaviour in future for fear of the consequences
- *rehabilitation*: the idea that the pupil will be helped to understand the moral wrongdoing of the misbehaviour and the need to behave well in future.

In schools, punishments often involve all three purposes to some extent, but rehabilitation is clearly the most important one and the one that embodies an educational purpose to enable a pupil to choose to behave well in future. Deterrence is also important and may contribute to the effectiveness of your expressions of disapproval when using reprimands. Retribution tends to be most evident when a moral code has been broken which the teacher feels needs to be punished in the interests of justice as an expression of the school community's disapproval, the most notable examples being bullying, stealing, cheating, vandalism and certain types of verbal abuse.

The shortcomings of punishment

The most important aspect of punishment to bear in mind is that its impact is largely dependent on it being used as a formal and weighty sanction employed for serious incidents of misbehaviour when other strategies have been unsuccessful. There is, however, an element of illusion involved here, since very few sanctions are in fact of any weight, with most involving only a short period of unpleasantness or having a nuisance value. Their impact owes much more to using them in a way that conveys the seriousness with which the misbehaviour is being viewed. It is also largely the case that the type of pupils most likely to be punished, notably dissaffected pupils who have little respect for authority and the values and ethos of the school, are the pupils least likely to respond by better behaviour in future. In contrast, those pupils who would be most worried about punishment are those for whom skilful use of other strategies should be sufficiently effective.

The main drawbacks to using punishments are:

- they form an inappropriate model for human relationships
- they foster anxiety and resentment
- they have a short-lived 'initial shock' effect
- they encourage pupils to develop strategies to avoid getting caught
- they do not promote good behaviour directly but simply serve to suppress misbehaviour
- they do not deal with the cause of the misbehaviour
- they focus attention on the misbehaviour.

Types of punishment

Despite the shortcomings of punishments, they do have a useful role to play in maintaining discipline if used skilfully. Each type of punishment has certain strengths and weaknesses which will have a bearing on their effectiveness. The most commonly used punishments are as follows.

Writing tasks.   These may range from writing out lines to a short essay on 'Why I misbehaved and will behave better in future'. The main advantage of this approach is that it is done in the pupil's own time without wasting yours. Its weakness is that it is often felt to have a patronising quality and is probably regarded as insulting by older pupils. It is essential not to require pupils to do work that is missing or overdue as part of their normal coursework as a punishment, since doing normal coursework should never be regarded as a punishment. Such a requirement must be explicitly justified on other grounds.

Detention.   This could entail keeping a pupil in detention for a break period or after school coupled with a writing task (as above), or simply detaining them in silence for a set period of time. Its main advantage is that it is widely disliked by pupils; its main disadvantage is that it can inconvenience you. It is essential to distinguish a detention from requiring to see a pupil for a period of time as part of an investigating and counselling approach or to issue a reprimand. A detention is a formal punishment and should be administered as such.

Loss of privileges.   This can range from requiring a pupil to sit alone and in isolation to preventing the pupil going on a school outing. Its main advantage is that it can be quite upsetting to the pupil; its main disadvantage that it can easily be seen as vindictive and unfair.

Exclusion from the class.   This can range from requiring the pupil to wait outside the classroom for a period of time to being sent to another classroom or place in the school. Its main advantage is that it removes the pupil from the classroom and allows them to think about why they were excluded; its main disadvantages are that it is not particularly unpleasant for some pupils and can pose other problems, such as a pupil who keeps looking in through a window or simply wanders off.

Verbal intimidation.   A very severe talking to may be considered as a punishment rather than a reprimand, particularly if done by a senior teacher in the school in a formal role as such. Its main advantages are that it can be very unpleasant and can be administered quickly; its main disadvantage is that it can provoke a confrontation. A severe talking to in this way should only take place in private.

Informing significant others.   Informing the headteacher or the pupil's parents is, for most pupils, very punishing. Its main advantage is that it is usually a quite powerful sanction; its main disadvantage is that the pupil may now feel labelled by the school as a disruptive pupil and may even feel the need to live up to this label as a result.

Symbolic punishment. Some schools have a system of recording bad conduct marks which translate into a detention for a given total and may be included on the school report to parents. Its main advantage is that it can use the formal ritual of punishment at a mild level; its main disadvantage is that it can be clumsy to administer and communicate.

Physical punishment. Not to be used.

Suspension from school. This is the ultimate sanction. It tends to be used as a final resort to help the pupil appreciate the immense gravity of the situation and the misbehaviour, either after a long history of problems or in reaction to a particular misbehaviour of the utmost seriousness (such as using drugs, or assaulting a teacher). For some, it provides the shock needed to salvage their school careers or acts as a vehicle for the provision of special support. For others, it marks a point of no return, and results in either transfer to another school, with perhaps a fresh start, or with pupils approaching the school leaving age, a limbo land during which efforts to place the pupil elsewhere are finally overtaken by time running out.

Effective use of punishments
While it is evident that punishments generally have a more severe and unpleasant consequence for a pupil than strategies based on investigating and counselling or using reprimands, that does not mean they are actually more powerful or effective in dealing with pupil misbehaviour. Indeed, in a survey of teachers' perceptions of the effectiveness of different strategies used to deal with difficult classes or pupils, conducted for the Elton Report (DES, 1989a), it was evident that while almost any strategy can be effective if used skilfully in the right situation, generally strategies based on reasoning with pupils were perceived as being the most effective. Indeed, recourse to a punishment in a situation may be counter-productive if all that might have been necessary and effective was offering some academic help or simply reasoning with the pupil. A major pitfall facing beginning teachers in particular, is to assume that a punishment is more powerful and hence more effective; as a result they resort to their use too readily and inappropriately.

The skilful and effective use of punishments involves a number of qualities, and include those qualities considered earlier in relation to the effective use of reprimands. There are, however, some additional qualities worthy of particular note.

Use sparingly.   Punishments should be used sparingly and judiciously, and in the vast majority of cases only after other strategies have been tried.

Timing.   Punishments should be given as soon as possible after the misbehaviour. If there is a long delay, the link should be re-established at the time given.

Tone.   A punishment should be conveyed as an expression of your just and severe disapproval of the misbehaviour, and given in the interests of the pupil and of the class as a whole. It should not result from you losing your temper or appear vindictive.

Fit the crime.   The type and severity of the punishment should be appropriate to the misbehaviour but should also take account of the context.

Due process.   It is important that the pupil accepts that the punishment is fair and just. This will normally mean that the pupil has been warned that such a consequence may follow, and that your expectations and actions regarding such misbehaviour are clear and consistent. The pupil should also be asked to explain the misbehaviour and encouraged to understand and accept why the punishment is just, deserved and appropriate.

Relates to school policy.   The punishment should relate to the overall policy of the school towards discipline.

Aversiveness.   The punishment must be unpleasant for the pupil. Some pupils may not mind being sent out of the room, or may even gain status in the eyes of peers in doing so. As such, each punishment needs to be of a type that is aversive for the pupil concerned and minimises any factors that are likely to weaken its effectiveness, bearing in mind the need to be fair and consistent.

It is also important to consult with colleagues in the school about any pupil giving cause for concern. If a pupil is having to be punished frequently, this may indicate an underlying problem which goes well beyond being the concern of the class teacher alone. While you may feel you are expected to cope with any discipline problems yourself as best you can, this does not mean it is desirable to keep problems to yourself as far as possible. In fact, the opposite is the case. You also have a responsibility towards pastoral care and you need to act as a member of a team in monitoring pupils' behaviour, so that any concerns you have are shared with others and appropriate action can then be better and more widely informed before decisions are taken.

Dealing with confrontations

From time to time a confrontation may develop in the classroom between you and a pupil. A confrontation may be characterised by a heated and emotional exchange, which is upsetting for all concerned. Such a confrontation can develop so quickly and unpredictably, that the first thing you are aware of is that you are in the middle of having one. Usually, however, there are warning signals evident that can enable you to pre-empt its development.

Triggers for confrontations
There are four major triggers for confrontation in the classroom:

- a pupil may feel emotional and tense as a result of prolonged learning difficulties which are causing increasing frustration
- a pupil may feel that the disciplinary strategy you are adopting towards them is unfair and constitutes a threat to their self-esteem, particularly if linked to loss of face in front of their peers (the use of sarcasm or ridicule may provoke this, or trying to resolve a conflict by making the pupil submit to your authority in some way, such as moving to a seat at the front of the classroom)
- a pupil may react against explicit physical or verbal intimidation, such as a teacher waving a finger in front of the pupil's face or using a forceful reprimand
- a pupil may be trying to avoid embarrassment when you are cajoling or insisting they answer a question or take part in an activity which they feel very anxious about or feel they may make a fool of themselves in front of others.

Clearly, skilful teaching and, in particular, the skilful use of the disciplinary strategies outlined earlier, will do much to minimise the occurrence of such triggers. However, there are circumstances which can lead to a pupil feeling over-sensitive to what otherwise would be unproblematic behaviour on your part. For example, there may be acute personal problems the pupil is having to deal with at home, or some upsetting news may have been received in school (eg being dropped from a school team, being told that their school report will be critical of poor progress, or even that a best friend has not invited the pupil to a party).

You can usually sense from the pupil's behaviour that something is amiss, such as the pupil looking tense or arriving in the classroom in an uncharacteristically loud manner. Such signals will alert you to the possibility that you may need to be sensitive to this in deciding how best to interact with the pupil.

Dealing with confrontations

If a confrontation does develop, there are some useful strategies that will enable you to deal successfully with the situation.

Stay calm.   If you remain calm, or regain your composure quickly, and interact calmly with the pupil, the pupil will quickly calm down.

Defuse the situation.   Rather than try to pursue the conflict further, you can tell the pupil that 'There's no need for anyone to get upset, I suggest you just calm down and we can deal with this at the end of the lesson' and then back off. If this is not effective, your best course of action is to send for help so that the pupil can be moved elsewhere for the rest of the lesson. Backing off in this way does not mean that you have backed down or lost authority. Indeed, it displays your skill in dealing with this as a special circumstance demanding appropriate action, and pupils will generally understand this. Some teachers can use humour to defuse a confrontation, but doing so successfully requires an adept sensitivity.

Be aware of the heat of the moment.   A confrontation can develop in a matter of seconds, and in the heat of the moment you or the pupil may say or do something which they may profoundly regret later. Bear this in mind before you act and in how you respond to what the pupil says or does.

Use your social skills.   A pupil may be horrified by what they have said or done but may lack the social skills to get out of the situation. It thus behoves you to use your social skills to help the pupil, for which they may be immensely grateful later once the incident is defused and dealt with.

Design a mutual face saver.   In the heat of the moment, your natural tendency may be to feel you must exert your authority by coming out 'on top' in some way. Such a stereotyped reaction is often unhelpful and counter-productive. You need to consider what strategy best fits the situation, and enables you and the pupil to come away from the incident with sufficient grace.

Get help if necessary. Do not hesitate to get assistance from another member of staff if this seems appropriate.

Research on how teachers deal with confrontations indicates that almost all confrontations can be avoided or resolved by the skilful use of conflict management techniques (eg Bowers, 1986). In particular, this requires teachers to be aware of their own emotions during conflicts and confrontations and how these might influence their behaviour, and to be able to stand outside the situation to think rationally about how best to proceed. The biggest danger facing you in dealing with a confrontation is to lose your temper or to see the situation as one where you have to come out on top by exerting any power you have. By remaining calm, standing back from the situation, thinking carefully, and using appropriate strategies skilfully, the vast majority of such incidents can be defused and dealt with efficiently and effectively, and without becoming unnecessarily unpleasant.

Other strategies

As well as the strategies outlined so far, there are some other strategies and approaches that are worthy of particular note.

Monitor your pupils' behaviour

Formal monitoring of behaviour

Formal procedures for monitoring pupils' behaviour can be effective. A frequently used strategy is to put a pupil 'on report', which means that for a period of a few days or a week, each teacher must make a note of the pupil's behaviour at the end of each teaching session on a report card. At the end of this period, the pupil's behaviour is reviewed.

Contingency contracting

The notion of 'contingency contracting' involves promising the pupil an agreed reward of some type if good behaviour is maintained over a specified period. The reward may typically be a merit certificate for good behaviour, allowing the pupil to spend time on a valued activity, such as an afternoon in the craft workshop, or even a tangible reward, such as a bar of chocolate. It is important to note that the real motivation here does not stem from the desire for the reward, but rather the desire to behave well. The procedure and reward simply serve as a helpful vehicle to support the pupil's own efforts.

Getting help from the parents

Enlisting the help of the pupil's parents is often very important if the behaviour has become a serious cause for concern. Parents should be informed about this, not only as part of the desirability of keeping parents informed in general about their children, but also because the parents may offer useful and helpful information themselves and assist in various ways to encourage an improvement in the pupil's behaviour. If it is suspected that the pupil may have a special educational need of some sort, the parents should be involved in any discussions at an early stage.

Units for disruptive pupils

Many schools are able to make use of on-site or off-site units to which disruptive pupils can be sent for a period or for certain timetabled lessons, as part of a cooling-off period during which the pupil can come to terms with the gravity of the situation and a plan can be agreed as to how best to proceed. At its best, this strategy can allow a crisis to be defused successfully followed by a return to normal schooling. At its worst, particularly for pupils near the school leaving age, it can result in *de facto* suspension.

Positive teaching

The above four strategies will normally be initiated by a senior member of staff in the school after wide consultation. The fifth strategy, however, can be used by a class teacher as an approach. It is that of 'positive teaching'. Positive teaching refers to an approach to classroom discipline based on ideas stemming from behavioural psychology. The basic underlying principle here is that pupil behaviour which is rewarded is more likely to occur in the same situation in future, and behaviour which is not rewarded or is punished, is less likely to occur.

Advocates of this approach to classroom teaching (eg Wheldall and Glynn, 1989), argue that it enables teachers to be more consistent, systematic and effective in how they deal with discipline problems. First, the teacher needs to identify desirable behaviours, which classroom rules will promote these, and which types of misbehaviour need to be dealt with. Having done this, you then use a programme of regularly praising and otherwise rewarding the desirable behaviours and reminding pupils of the classroom rules. The important point about this approach is its emphasis on the use of praise and other rewards to encourage and sustain improved behaviour. Punishments are rarely used. Rather, the teacher is careful to ensure that praising and other rewards do not follow misbehaviour. Research studies based on evaluating this approach indicate that its skilful use can successfully improve the behaviour of the class as a whole and also promote better behaviour with individual pupils causing problems (Wheldall and Glynn, 1989).

Key questions about your discipline

1 Is my discipline embedded within a positive classroom climate characterised by mutual respect and rapport and positive expectations, and linked with good lesson presentation and management?

2 Is my authority established and accepted by pupils?

3 Am I clear and consistent in establishing rules and expectations regarding pupils' behaviour?

4 Do I make good use of general teaching skills and pre-emptive strategies to minimise pupil misbehaviour occurring?

5 Do I make good use of investigating and counselling strategies, reprimands and punishments, to deal with pupil misbehaviour skilfully?

6 Are the strategies I use to deal with pupil misbehaviour employed flexibly and skilfully to take account of which strategy is likely to be most effective and appropriate to the situation?

7 Do my disciplinary strategies encourage good behaviour without undermining a positive classroom climate?

8 Do I avoid confrontations where possible, and efficiently and effectively defuse those which occur?

9 Am I sufficiently sensitive to my pastoral care role and alert to any particular needs of individual pupils giving cause for concern?

10 Do I make adequate use of consultation with colleagues and ensure that my actions complement the school's general policy towards discipline?

7 Assessing pupils' progress

The regular assessment of pupils' progress is part and parcel of teaching and learning in the classroom. Such assessment may range from simply looking over pupils' shoulders while they are writing during a period of normal classwork, to the use of formally administered external examinations. Indeed, there is a vast variety of activities used to assess pupils' progress, each with their own particular processes and procedures. Nevertheless, the skilful use of assessment techniques can be identified, and these will be highlighted in this chapter.

The purposes of assessment

In essence, assessment refers to any activity used to appraise pupils' performance. The learning outcomes promoted by schools concern helping pupils to develop knowledge, understanding, skills and attitudes. Assessment thus refers to techniques you can use to monitor pupils' progress in terms of specific learning outcomes. The first and most important question facing you in assessing pupils' progress, is why? What purpose have you in mind for the assessment activity?

Assessment can serve a number of different purposes. The most frequently used purposes are as follows.

1 *To provide you with feedback about pupils' progress.* Such feedback enables you to consider how effective your teaching has been in achieving its intended learning outcomes. In particular, it may highlight certain problems or misunderstandings that have arisen, that will require remedial action in your subsequent teaching.
2 *To provide pupils with educative feedback.* Assessment enables pupils to relate their performance to the standard expected, to use detailed feedback to correct and improve their work, and to appreciate more clearly the requirements of the tasks set (eg regarding the layout of the work or procedures used).
3 *To motivate pupils.* Assessment activities can act as a spur to pupils to organise their work well and to learn what is required so as to achieve well at these activities. The spur may be largely based on intrinsic motivation, extrinsic motivation, or a

balance of both. Feedback of success at a challenging task is particularly effective in stimulating future motivation.

4 *To provide a record of progress.* Regular assessment activities enable you to keep a record of pupils' progress over a long period. This can then form the basis for your decisions about individual pupils' current and future educational needs, particularly if a cause for concern arises. It can also be used when communicating with others, including parents, and may influence your future planning of teaching similar groups.

5 *To provide a statement of current attainment.* A specific assessment activity or group of activities can be used to identify the standard of attainment achieved at a particular point in time. Such attainment may form the basis of certification, or a formal statement issued to others, most notably parents.

6 *To assess pupils' readiness for future learning.* Assessment can be used to indicate whether pupils are ready for a particular type of learning (eg readiness to learn to read), whether a particular ability grouping may be appropriate, whether they have any specific learning difficulties, or, more simply, whether they have covered the previous learning required for the new topic to be taught effectively (if not, revision or prior preparation will be needed).

Your decisions about how and what to assess will thus depend on the exact purpose or purposes you have in mind for the assessment. Part of the difficulty facing teachers in making skilful and effective use of assessment, is the need to meet different purposes and uses of assessment at the same time, and to ensure that any undesirable side-effects are avoided or limited so far as possible.

Dangers of assessment

There are three major dangers that need to be guarded against when making use of assessment activities. First, and most serious of all, is the danger that pupils who find that the feedback concerning their progress indicates they are doing less well than peers or some standard of attainment of value to them, may become disheartened and upset by this. This may lead to them becoming disenchanted and alienated from schooling, and sinking into a vicious cycle of increasing under-achievement. Second, the procedures and practices adopted for assessing pupils' progress may be too time-consuming and bureaucratic for teachers and pupils, such that it encroaches undesirably on time and energy that could be better spent on other activities. Third, it may lead teachers and pupils to becoming over-concerned with pupils performing well. In particular, assessment activities that the curriculum offers to pupils (both in terms of content and in terms of teaching and learning processes involved) may become geared to success at the expense of the quality of educational experiences occurring in the classroom.

Because assessment practices are so inter-linked with teaching and learning, the skilful use of assessment practices which complement and facilitate the hallmarks of effective teaching considered in previous chapters, is essential. Where assessment practices are used which have undesirable side-effects, these can make it much more difficult to teach effectively. Indeed, many of the reforms in assessment practices over the years have stemmed precisely from a recognition of the important role of assessment in promoting effective teaching.

Types of assessment

As a result of the diversity in the type of assessment practices used in schools, a number of key terms are now frequently referred to. The most important of these are as follows.

Formative assessment. Assessment aimed to promote effective further learning by pupils. It may do this by giving the pupil helpful feedback, or by giving you feedback or information that will enable you to meet the pupil's future learning needs more effectively. Typically, such assessment tends to identify errors, difficulties or shortcomings in the pupil's work and offer advice, guidance and information to improve future performance.

Summative assessment. Assessment which identifies the standard of attainment achieved at a particular moment in time, normally carried out at the end of a period of instruction (eg end of term, end of course). The most typical examples are the grades used on school reports of attainment, or the results of external examinations.

Norm-referenced assessment. The grading of each pupil's performance in relation to the performance of others. For example, if a grade A is defined as the level of attainment achieved by the top ten per cent of the assessment cohort, this would mean that no matter how high or low the general standard of work produced was, the best ten per cent would always receive a grade A.

Criterion-referenced assessment. The grading of each pupil's performance in terms of whether a particular description of performance (the criterion) has been met. This means that all pupils who meet this criterion would be assessed as achieving the related grade, regardless of how other pupils performed. Typical examples of these are graded tests used in music, modern languages and mathematics, the use of grade-related criteria at GCSE, and the levels of attainment in the National Curriculum (eg see Desforges, 1989; Selkirk, 1988).

Diagnostic assessment. This overlaps with formative assessment, but specifically identifies learning difficulties or problems. Certain tests can be used to identify particular needs, and related to the statements of special educational needs.

Internal assessment. Assessment activities which are devised, carried out and marked by the class teachers, and often used as part of their own programme of teaching.

External assessment. Assessment activities devised by examiners outside the school, and usually also marked by external assessors, although in many cases marking can be done by the class teachers but is then checked ('moderated') by external assessors on a sample basis.

Informal assessment. Assessment based on the observation of performance which occurs in the classroom as part of normal classroom practice.

Formal assessment. Assessment made following prior warning that an assessment will be carried out. This normally allows the pupil an opportunity to revise and prepare for the assessment.

Continuous assessment. Basing the final assessment of the standard of attainment achieved on pieces of assessment made over a long period of time.

Terminal assessment. Basing the final assessment of the standard of attainment achieved on an assessment made solely at the end of the course or programme of work.

Objective assessment. Assessment activities and associated marking schemes having extremely high agreement between assessors on the marks awarded. The best example of this is the use of multiple-choice tests.

Process assessment. Assessment of an on-going activity, such as reading aloud a poem or designing and conducting an experiment, in which the assessment is based on direct observation of the performance while in progress.

Product assessment. Assessment based on a tangible piece of work, such as an essay, project, drawing, model, or examination script, submitted for that purpose.

Discussion about types of assessment typically considers contrasting pairs, most notably:

- formative versus summative
- norm-referenced versus criterion-referenced
- internal versus external
- informal versus formal
- continuous versus terminal
- process versus product.

While this is often helpful, the nature of assessment practices is often such that a mixture of each contrasting pair is in fact involved. Thus, for example, one may imagine that an end of year school report was primarily a summative assessment, but inspection of its contents may reveal many comments and pieces of information clearly intended to be formative. Similarly, an assessment scheme for marking a coursework project may claim to be primarily criterion-referenced, but close inspection may reveal aspects that are clearly norm-referenced. In tailoring your assessment practice to the purpose you have in mind, it is most important that the assessment is effective in meeting the needs you have for it. Over-concern with its purity, in terms of pigeon-holing its type, is likely to be unproductive.

Improving assessment practices
Looking at the types of assessments listed above, and bearing in mind the range of *learning outcomes* that can be assessed (knowledge, understanding, skills and attitudes), the *type and nature of the performance* involved (oral, written, practical, coursework, tests, examinations) and the *educational domains* (the various academic subjects, study skills including reading, writing and organisational skills, and personal and social skills such as motivation and the ability to work well as part of a group), it is perhaps not surprising that a number of complex issues underlie the skilful assessment of pupils' progress.

Much has been written about assessment practices in schools and the need for various reforms. For example, Weston (1989) has noted five major negative aspects of current assessment practices:

- an emphasis on norm-referenced assumptions, which results in pupils who find the work difficult being destined to receive low marks and to see themselves as failures
- an emphasis on summative assessment, leading to the reporting of results that offer little help to pupils in understanding their difficulties or on how to improve
- an emphasis on a cognitive, content-based, academic curriculum,

which has high status, but fails to recognise other important types of achievement
- pupils being passive receivers of assessment practices, with little say in the process involved or awareness of the criteria being used
- the aggregation of pupils' achievements, such that particular achievements and difficulties are masked, which reduces the information content of the summative statement produced.

As such, Weston argues that there are six major directions for improving assessment practices:

- more emphasis on formative assessment
- assessing more aspects of achievement
- better specification of learning targets
- more individualised pacing of learning
- involving the pupil as a partner in assessment
- forms of certification which ensure progression towards worthwhile training after compulsory schooling.

Recent developments

Interestingly, however, a number of recent developments in assessment practices in both primary and secondary schools are in line with just these directions; for example, the move towards greater assessment of practical work (eg APU, 1989), greater use of diagnostic assessment (eg Mason, 1989), and the major developments associated with pupil profiling and records of achievement (DES, 1988b), GCSE (see Selkirk, 1988), and most notably of all, with the National Curriculum (DES, 1988a; Whetton, 1989). Alongside all these developments, it is also important to note that tensions can arise between the different purposes and practices of assessment now commonly in use, particularly when constraints on time and resources necessitate trying to meet different needs at the same time. Given the major influence that assessment practices have on both teachers' and pupils' behaviour (see Crooks, 1988), resolving such tensions successfully is no mean task.

Indeed, Troman (1989) has raised a number of concerns about the National Curriculum regarding the tension between the use of formative assessment carried out by teachers and the external testing at ages 7, 11, 14 and 16. Troman argues that whereas the former is largely developmental and concerned with fostering pupils' educational progress, the latter is bound up with the monitoring of standards and provides a basis for monitoring individual schools' relative effectiveness. In effect, the tension generated is very much that of a clash between two distinct cultures.

Assessment activities in the classroom

As discussed earlier, assessment activities are going on in schools all the time, ranging from asking pupils questions during normal classwork, to administering a formal written examination. In carrying out assessment activities, you need to be clear about the main purpose or purposes of the assessment and the type of assessment you want to use, as has been considered so far in this chapter. After this, you are then ready to think about how best to select, design and carry out the appropriate assessment activities themselves.

The main assessment activities in use in the classroom are:

- monitoring normal classwork activities
- designated assessment tasks integrated within normal classwork
- homework
- assessment tests designed by the teacher
- standardised tests
- formal examinations.

You should use a wide range of assessment activities

Monitoring normal classwork activities

Monitoring normal classwork activities is a central aspect of teaching, and is bound up with your decision-making about the progress of the lesson and the feedback you give to pupils to facilitate their learning. The most important aspects of such assessment are that you ensure that you monitor all pupils' progress regularly (not just those who frequently demand or require more attention). Furthermore, your monitoring should be investigative and active, in the sense that you actively probe pupils' current understanding and difficulties rather than simply rely on this being drawn to your attention in some way. Many forms of assessment in common use now, involve teachers noting performance by pupils occurring as part of normal classwork.

Designated assessment tasks integrated within normal classwork

It is a thin line between monitoring normal classwork activities and using designated assessment tasks integrated within normal classwork. Some activities that need to be assessed occur in normal classwork on a regular basis, whereas others need to be specifically designed and introduced for the purpose of the assessment. The latter is often the case if it is important for the task to be carefully standardised and assessed in terms of specific criteria that require close attention. In either case, however, you need to consider whether you should forewarn pupils that a particular assessment activity is to take place and indicate its purpose and use. Skilful assessment of pupils' progress in meeting the National Curriculum attainment targets depends very much on how well assessment tasks are integrated within normal classwork without disrupting or interfering unduly with the normal progress of learning.

Homework

The use of homework tasks is very important in providing feedback concerning how well a pupil can perform when unaided. Homework is particularly useful in developing pupils' organisational skills and power of commitment to meet the demands made on them. It can also provide stark feedback to the pupil and to you of the nature of any difficulties or problems that arise which are less evident in the class where you may be readily available to provide help. Unfortunately, in this respect, parental help is both useful in providing further tuition, but also unhelpful if it readily enables the pupil to enlist assistance rather than persevere with their own efforts. Parental help has also posed problems for the assessment of independent project work done partly or largely at home, and much such work now has to be based solely on classwork activity.

While it is common for homework to be used to assess pupils' previous learning in lessons, and as such, often involves consolidation and practice-type tasks, or to prepare for a test by revising, it is important to use homework to good effect by encouraging new learning. This involves not simply the learning of new material, but also the creative investigation and application of the topic area to life outside the school (eg listing cubes, spheres and cylinders that can be found in your living room, or exploring the earliest recollections of the pupil's parents about when they first went to school).

Assessment tests designed by the teacher

Short tests devised by you can motivate learning in preparation for the test, and provide a formal note of attainment in the test. Regular tests can be particularly useful in conveying the importance of making progress with new learning, but can also be very threatening. As such they have to be used with sensitivity and in a way that will facilitate rather than discourage learning. Short tests vary immensely in type and form, ranging from a spelling test based on homework, to an end-of-course or topic test used to assess academic progress.

Standardised tests

Standardised tests are widely used to monitor progress and attainment in key areas of learning, most notably reading, but also in a range of language tasks, mathematics, and as part of screening procedures to identify pupils who may have special educational needs. Such tests are useful in enabling the teacher to compare the result with that expected for a pupil of that age. In using standardised tests, however, you must be alert to their appropriateness for the use you are making of them. In particular, a dated test may well include words, formats or tasks which are no longer commonly used. A mathematics test may explore attainment based on a different coverage or approach to the one your pupils have experienced. In addition, a test result, of course, can only be based on what was tested, which means that other aspects of performance which may be difficult to test are largely excluded. Given the increasing diversity of learning skills and qualities being fostered in schools, written tests in particular are likely to be inadequate as the major or sole assessment activity used to measure attainment.

Formal examinations

Formal examinations devised by the school for the purpose of internal assessment are relatively rare in primary schools but commonplace in secondary schools. The formality varies from classroom-based examinations designed and administered by the class teacher at an appropriate time, to examinations designed in collaboration and administered as part of an examination timetable. As well as providing a useful measure of attainment to be used in school reports, they also help develop examination skills and techniques, and prepare pupils for external examinations, most notably at age 16.

Carrying out assessment activities

In carrying out assessment activities, a number of important points need to be borne in mind:

- the assessment activity must be a fair one, in the sense of re-lating to the work covered, so that pupils can be reasonably expected to perform well on the activity if progress has been made during the appropriate coursework
- the assessment activity should relate to the learning outcomes planned by the school; these may be documented in terms of appropriate aspects of the National Curriculum or as part of a particular course of study detailing a syllabus, content and assessment criteria to be achieved
- the programme of assessment activities used over a long period should be varied in type and form so that the full range of learning outcomes intended are assessed and that these are assessed in different ways
- pupils should be informed about the nature and purpose of assessment activities, how they are used, and the criteria em-ployed that characterise successful performance
- the conduct of assessment activities should facilitate perform-ance by taking place in appropriate circumstances, and, in particular, avoiding disruptions and, so far as possible, mini-mising pupils' anxieties
- assessment activities should be carefully designed to ensure that tasks are unambiguous and the type and nature of performance expected is clear to pupils
- most importantly of all, you need to ensure that the assessment activity actually assesses validly what it is intended to assess.

Skills underlying assessment
Three examples will suffice to illustrate the complex skills needed to carry out assessment activities effectively. The first concerns designing a multiple-choice test in science.

'In very cold weather pipes sometimes burst because?'
(a) Water expands when it freezes.
(b) Ice is harder than water.
(c) Unlagged pipes always burst.
(d) Cold water softens pipes.

In designing this item, the teacher needs to check that the question is clear and appropriate, and that the four options will effectively discriminate between pupils who have the understanding being tested from those who do not. You also need to consider whether this test item is a good example of the particular learning outcome being assessed: knowledge, understanding, ability to relate science to real-life applications, appreciation of the notion of cause and effect, or whatever.

A second example comes from a document to be completed by secondary school pupils taking part in a paired-reading scheme at a primary school as a component of a community studies unit. (Paired reading involves the older pupil listening to the younger pupil's reading.) The following section appears within the self-assessment section:

'When you have finished your module, we would like you to give a summary of your experience (please ring round the words to answer the questions).'
1 I felt the help I gave in reading was:
   useless, easy, exciting, useful, dull, enjoyable, difficult.
2 Do you think your attitude and behaviour was?:
   responsible, unhelpful, helpful, wasting time.
3 Do you feel proud that you have done your best?:
   yes, no.
4 Would you like to do this type of thing again?:
   yes, no.

In designing this assessment activity, the teacher clearly needs to think about its purpose, whether it will do what it is intended to do effectively, and how it will be used. In particular, were the pupils involved in the design of this self-assessment section and informed of its purpose and use, and how will it be related to other evidence of their performances?

The third example is asking a class of junior school age pupils to write a short story about a woman who fell into a river. Such a task could be used to assess a whole range of aspects concerning progress in writing, including technical aspects such as handwriting, grammar, punctuation and use of capital letters, and aspects of its content, such as creativity, use of ideas, and intelligibility to the reader. Because the same assessment task can be used for different areas of evaluation, it is often important to indicate to pupils which aspect is being assessed. Thus, for example, you could tell pupils to try to make the story as imaginative as possible, as this is the aspect you are assessing (as such, a very imaginative story should still get a high mark even if there are technical shortcomings).

It will be evident from consideration of these three examples, that carrying out assessment activities involves a whole range of skills regarding selection, design, implementation, match of activity to purpose, marking procedures, feedback, and appropriate and valid use of the results of the assessment.

Marking, recording and reporting

A number of studies and reports concerning assessment practices in primary and secondary schools have highlighted the importance of sound and appropriate practice regarding the marking of pupils' work and the recording and reporting of pupils' progress (eg Bennett *et al*, 1984; Crooks, 1988; HMI, 1988a; Mortimore *et al*, 1988). Crooks (1988), in particular, has noted the great impact that such practice can have, for good or ill, on pupils' perceptions about their own progress and their future behaviour concerning motivation, strategies and prioritising for further learning.

Marking normal coursework

The marking of pupils' work during and after lessons needs to be thorough and constructive, and returned in good time. Good practice in marking acts as an important model for pupils in setting them an example of the care and attention that needs to be devoted towards academic tasks, and can thereby maintain a high expectation for the standard of work required. The formative aspect of marking is of fundamental importance to effective teaching and learning. Feedback that enables the pupil to make further progress by understanding more clearly what needs to be done can enhance motivation and self-confidence. For example, receiving a low mark for the imaginative quality of an essay or for a description of an experimental procedure without any guidance as to how the work could have been improved, will tend to dishearten. Constructive and helpful guidance on how a better piece of work could have been produced, however, will help stimulate further progress.

The marking of pupils' work completed as part of normal class-work and homework tasks is simply an extension of the normal process of teaching and learning. The major challenge facing you in marking pupils' work, is how to be helpful and encouraging for the whole range of attainment in the class. The main problem is that norm-referenced marking, based on comparing the work of pupils with each other, will tend to discourage the lower attainers. As such, most teachers try to make greater use of marking related to attainment standards expected of each pupil taking account of previous progress. In this respect, good use can be made of tasks which are more clearly matched to each pupil's ability (as is the case with many workcard schemes) or using tasks which are graded in terms of increasing difficulty. In addition, you may decide to keep the written record of marks in your own record books but not report these to pupils. Instead, your feedback to pupils will take the form of comments about the work, and areas of improvement which are required. It is also important to give feedback about effort, if you feel a pupil has done less well or better than expected as a result of their efforts. Indeed, many schools give a mark for effort as well as attainment in relation to the assessment of normal coursework.

It is also useful to make use of a variety of marking methods, including allowing pupils to mark their own work or each other's from time to time. In addition, marks over a period of time should also be based on a variety of assessment activities to ensure that the run of marks reflects different aspects of attainment. The most important function of marking to bear in mind is that it should provide helpful and encouraging feedback to pupils about their progress. Part of this may mean that pupils will need help in thinking about their study skills and how they organise their work so that they can better prepare for such assessment tasks in future.

Marking formal assessment tasks

As well as marking normal classwork and homework, you will also be marking a whole range of formal assessment tasks, including tests and examinations. The skills involved in such marking have become increasingly complex with the growth of more detailed marking practices. Performance in a subject or area of the curriculum is now typically divided into a number of components or elements, and the marking scheme is devised so that the mark awarded on a particular aspect of performance is clearly related to the component or element being assessed. This enables attainment to be recorded in terms of a profile of components rather than as an overall single mark or grade, or if the latter is the case, the single mark or grade is based on a specified weighting of the different components involved.

As such, the marking of formal assessment tasks involves careful consideration, not so much of the correctness of the pupil's performance, but rather a judgement of what the quality of the performance indicates. The National Curriculum specifies for each subject area a number of Attainment Targets, which together make up the knowledge, understanding and skills that comprise increasing educational attainment. Each Attainment Target is divided into a number of levels of increasing attainment. Designing and marking the associated assessment tasks thus requires a clear appreciation of how performance relates to a specific level of attainment on the Attainment Target being assessed. Thus, for example, the statement of attainment in science for Attainment Target 4 (Genetics and evolution) level 4, requires pupils to be able to measure variations in living organisms. As such, the assessment task or tasks used must match this statement, by taking account of what type of pupil performance would exemplify such attainment. Doing this needs to reflect a clear understanding of what the statement means, how it relates to progression in the Attainment Target from lower levels to higher levels, and devising a mark scheme for performance which is fair, reliable, valid and practical.

Marking personal qualities and attitudes

The assessment of personal qualities and attitudes has always posed problems of reliability and validity. While most teachers form impressionistic judgements about these, some forms of assessment, such as records of achievement, have demanded that such judgements be based on performance related to particular tasks where a fair opportunity to display particular qualities or attitudes (such as acting responsibly, showing initiative, working conscientiously when unsupervised) can be given. Again, it is important to prepare pupils for such assessment and to discuss with them what is expected, and how marks or grades are achieved.

Recording pupils' progress

The need for teachers to keep good records of pupils' progress has been emphasized frequently by the HMI in their inspections of schools (eg HMI, 1987). However, it is also important to recognise that the usefulness of keeping records is dependent on the extent to which the records are in fact used. Keeping records that are much too detailed or in a form that serves little purpose will not be a good use of your time.

Keep thorough records of your pupils' progress

Keeping a good record of pupils' progress should serve three main functions:

- it should provide a useful basis from which reports to others (eg the pupils themselves, parents, other teachers) can be made
- it should highlight any cause for concern if a pupil's performance shows a marked drop compared with previous progress
- it should facilitate the planning of future work with each pupil by building upon previous progress and, in particular, by ensuring that progress is adequate in its breadth and depth of coverage and that areas requiring remedial work receive attention.

In addition, such records can usefully contribute to the school's general decision-making about programmes of study. In this respect, notes about the work covered, including samples of pupils' work and test scores, can help to ensure that the curriculum provided each year matches pupils' needs and abilities adequately.

Reporting pupils' progress

Feedback to pupils about their progress is of immense importance in contributing to motivation and further progress, as has been noted already. In addition, however, you also need to report on pupils' progress on a regular basis to parents, either in the form of written reports and/or during meetings with them.

Written reports to parents have been the subject of much debate. Goacher and Reid (1983) noted that teachers' comments about pupils in such reports could be grouped into 15 main areas: ability, attitude to subject, behaviour, confidence, effort, examination results, homework, progress, maturity, participation, presentation of written work, future performance, suggestions for improvement, attendance and pastoral comments. Child (1986) has listed five problems that face teachers in writing school reports:

- one often has to rely on subjective judgements, which some teachers find uncomfortable
- it is difficult to summarise performance in different parts of the subject or curriculum area in a concise form that is adequate and meaningful to the reader
- there is a tension between giving honest reports and not being demoralising if the comments are critical or reflect low attainment
- it is often difficult to know which aspect of a pupil's performance warrants being highlighted in the report
- some teachers may find it difficult to remember adequately every pupil taught.

Writing reports that are fair, valid, meaningful to the reader, and have a positive effect on future progress, involves a number of skills. As well as making good use of your knowledge about each pupil and your records of progress, you need to make comments that are helpful and constructive. Where you need to be critical, this should usefully point to what needs to be done in future to improve matters.

In general, studies of parents' views about school reports indicate that they would like school reports more often than is typical at present (annually or twice-yearly written reports and/or meetings being the most common pattern) and would like more information than is normally given. Clearly, there is tension here between parents, quite naturally, wanting more frequent and more detailed reports, and the additional demands that this would place on schools. Reporting pupils' progress in terms of the National Curriculum Attainment Targets provides a basis that allows for a more detailed reporting to take place within a clearly defined framework for describing attainment and progress, which may address some of these concerns.

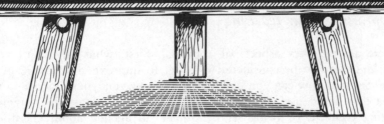

Key questions about your assessment of pupils' progress

1 Do I make use of an appropriate variety of assessment activities?

2 Do I make use of the various purposes for assessment, including both formative and summative purposes and also as a means of monitoring the success of my own teaching and future planning?

3 Do I ensure that each assessment activity is well-tailored to the purpose for which it is intended?

4 Is my marking of assessment tasks and feedback to pupils sufficiently speedy, thorough, constructive and helpful, so as to foster and sustain pupils' motivation and self-confidence and facilitate further progress?

5 Do I help pupils to prepare for assessment tasks so as to enable them to achieve success by having a clear understanding of the expectations required and how these can best be achieved?

6 Are the assessment activities I use fair in terms of being well-matched to the work covered and to pupils' abilities, and in terms of being valid indicators of the learning outcomes being monitored?

7 Are the assessment activities carried out in a way that will facilitate achievement?

8 Do I help develop pupils' ability to evaluate their own progress through the use of self-assessment activities?

9 Are my records of pupils' progress based on a variety of types of assessment activities and different aspects of performance, and are they well-suited to the purposes for which the records are kept?

10 Are my reports to parents, and others, fair and informative?

8 Reflection and evaluation

All teachers spend a great deal of time reflecting about and evaluating how well they are performing their work, both with particular regard to their classroom teaching and with regard to other aspects of their work in general. Reflection and evaluation is inherent in the job. It is impossible to meet the various demands of teaching without planning, organising, monitoring and evaluating the activities you carry out. What differs between teachers, however, is how skilfully and systematically they carry this out.

In recent years, this quality of critically thinking about your own performance in the classroom, often referred to as 'reflective teaching' (see Calderhead, 1989; Pollard and Tann, 1987), has been widely advocated by, amongst others, the HMI (eg HMI, 1985), as needing to be fostered and encouraged as part of teachers' normal practice and professional development.

All teachers do this in an intuitive and ad hoc way most of the time. In addition, however, some teachers have also been involved in more systematic self-appraisal processes, either as part of a specific scheme of self-evaluation within the school, or as part of a network of teachers who have been involved in researching aspects of their own practice within the teacher action research movement (see HMI, 1985; Hustler *et al*, 1986). More recently, the move towards identifying teacher competencies and the introduction of formal schemes for teacher appraisal has led to many teachers being involved in systematically appraising their own classroom practice (see DES, 1989c; Turner and Clift, 1988).

This chapter focuses on the skills involved in evaluating your own current teaching practice in order to improve your future practice. As well as exploring self-appraisal, this will also consider how you can help your colleagues and how your colleagues can help you in carrying out this task to best effect.

Appraising your teaching

There are two key aspects of appraisal. First, what aspects of your teaching need to be considered in order to improve your future practice? Second, how can you best go about improving your practice in the area that could usefully be developed? The first aspect thus involves setting yourself, or being set by others, an agenda about classroom teaching to consider, and then collecting some data that will enable you, or others, to judge the area that could usefully be developed. The second aspect deals with the programme for development.

Setting an agenda for classroom teaching

Setting the initial agenda for your classroom teaching can be done in a number of ways. Studies of teacher self-evaluation indicate that most teachers tend to take as their starting point some problem that they are concerned about, rather than attempt to formally review their teaching as a whole. For example, a teacher may feel that they ought to make greater use of group work activities, or that coursework activities need to be more clearly planned, or that too many pupils in the class become restless and inattentive during lessons. Such concerns may lead the teacher to explore carefully their own current practice with a view to considering how best to improve future practice. This process would constitute the first part of a teacher action research strategy, which would then lead on to devising a solution to improve practice, implementing the solution, and then evaluating its success.

Teachers who attempt to review their teaching as a whole are usually involved in a formal scheme of some sort, in which a checklist of questions about current practice or a set of rating scales are used. For example, the following list of statements is fairly typical, and I have used them in workshops on teacher self-assessment with student teachers and experienced teachers. The teachers are asked to rate themselves on each statement as 'I am happy with this aspect of my teaching' or 'I think I could usefully look at this aspect further'. The statements are:

1 I plan my lessons well, with clear aims and a suitable lesson content and structure.
2 I prepare the materials needed for the lessons, such as worksheets and apparatus, in good time.
3 My explanations and instructions are clear and pitched at the right level for pupils to understand.
4 I distribute questions around the classroom well and use both open and closed questions.
5 I use a variety of learning activities.
6 My lessons are suitable for the range of ability of pupils in the class (able, average and less able).
7 I maintain a level of control and order that is conducive for learning to occur.
8 I monitor pupils' learning closely during the lesson and give help to those having difficulties.
9 I mark work, including homework, thoroughly, constructively and in good time.

10 I have good relationships with pupils based on mutual respect and rapport.
11 My subject expertise is fine for the work I do.

In order to help ensure that teachers are honest in using this list of statements, they are told that it is for their own personal use simply to help them think about which area of their teaching they might like to focus on in considering their classroom teaching. It is useful to note that the second rating category does not imply that by wanting to look at this aspect further, your current practice is unsatisfactory. This is essential, since the need for change in your teaching often has nothing to do with your current practice being weak. Change does not mean that your previous practice was wrong. Not appreciating this point has caused many teachers faced with the need to change much unnecessary anguish.

Rating scales

As well as such checklists, many teachers have made use of more sophisticated rating scales in the role of appraiser when observing the teaching of a colleague. Such classroom observation instruments vary greatly in format and content, and in particular whether the rating scale is norm-referenced (eg above average, average, below average) or criterion-referenced (*viz* describes the behaviour indicative of each category on the rating scale), or a judgemental and ambiguous mixture of both (eg excellent, good, satisfactory, unsatisfactory).

There is no definitive description of what constitutes effective teaching, as was noted in Chapter 1; as such, a whole variety of different classroom observation instruments have been used to explore classroom practice. Indeed, the report evaluating the teacher appraisal pilot study (Cambridge Institute of Education, 1989) noted that observers differed in both the type of observation schedules they used (including some who used no schedule at all) and in their style of observation (including some who helped with the teaching while appraising).

Using an agreed list of teacher competencies

The move by the DES towards defining the key teacher competencies together with their descriptions may well lead to greater uniformity in teacher appraisal schemes, and in the type and way that classroom observation schemes are used. Unfortunately, one major drawback over using a list of competencies, is that it tends to emphasize the summative assessment aspect of appraisal rather than the formative aspect. This thereby implies that the aim of appraisal is to identify weaknesses that need development. As was noted earlier, however, most teachers' need to develop their classroom practice is more to do with the need to meet new demands stemming from changes in the curriculum and patterns of teaching, learning and assessment, rather than to correct weaknesses. Teacher appraisal schemes must emphasize the formative aspect of appraisal and provide a supportive ethos which will foster and encourage teachers' own reflection and evaluation about their classroom teaching if such schemes are to facilitate teachers' efforts to monitor and develop their own practice.

One advantage of using a nationally agreed description of teacher competencies is that it would aid the monitoring of teachers' development from initial training, through the probationary year and induction period, and into their careers as experienced teachers. Indeed, the DES has already attempted to define the teacher competencies expected at the end of initial training through the CATE criteria (the criteria used by the Council for the Accreditation of Teacher Education to approve the content of initial teacher training courses). This may well link up with the teacher competencies it expects experienced teachers to develop. Establishing a bridge between the two is high on the educational agenda (see Whitty, 1990). As such, the CATE criteria which relate to classroom teaching listed below (DES, 1989b) reflect the DES' view of some of the teacher competencies expected to develop during initial training and to be further developed during the first few years of teaching:

1 Manage children individually, in groups and as a whole class so that work is carried out in a responsible and orderly manner.
2 Differentiate work according to the range of abilities and attainments within a given teaching group or class.
3 Employ a range of teaching methods appropriate to a whole class, groups or individuals.
4 Match teaching methods to the learning activity and pay due attention to pace.
5 Establish good working relationships with classes and individual pupils.
6 Communicate clearly and intelligently with pupils orally and in writing.
7 Evaluate the effectiveness of their teaching in the light of pupils' responses and make appropriate adjustments.

Whatever the circumstances are in which you come to appraise your classroom teaching, whether self-initiated or as part of a formal scheme of appraisal, and whether using a list of teacher competencies and some type of observation schedule or not, you will need to consider detailed information about aspects of your teaching if you are to base your plans for further development on a systematic analysis of your current practice. Collecting and receiving such feedback is the area we turn to next.

Collecting data about your current practice

During a period when there are major changes in the curriculum relating to patterns of teaching, learning and assessment, it is all too obvious where you might feel you need to develop your practice. It may be that as a primary school teacher you need to develop your teaching of science or history topics, or as a secondary school teacher to develop your teaching of investigational work in mathematics or assessment of coursework tasks in English. However, much important reflection and evaluation concerns you thinking about your teaching that you are broadly happy with and yet feel could usefully be developed in some way. It is in exploring your current practice when there is no obvious problem that collecting data in some way can be very helpful.

Methods of data collection
There are a variety of ways in which you can collect data about your current practice. One or more of the following methods are likely to be the most useful.

Writing a diary.   This may be done after each lesson with a particular class or classes or alternatively at the end of each school day. It can be

Collect as much information as you can about your classroom practice

particularly useful in helping you to clarify the nature of your concerns and in noting particular incidents which are examples of the concern.

Making a recording of your lessons. This may be done using an audiotape or a videotape. The main advantage of such recording is that their detail enables you to highlight aspects of your teaching which, during the busyness of the actual lessons, you are unaware of as being worthy of attention and development.

Getting feedback from a colleague observing your lessons. This is an essential feature of formal schemes of teacher appraisal, but has also featured widely in many informal co-operative activities amongst teachers exploring their own practice. Feedback from an observer appears to work best when you brief your observer about the aspect of your teaching you want feedback on, and when such feedback is descriptive (*viz* describes what happened) rather than judgemental. Judgemental feedback is also valuable, but great care needs to be taken to ensure that the judgements come from a trusted observer, occurs in a supportive and non-threatening context, and is fair. Interestingly, observers often claim to learn as much, if not more, about their own teaching from observing colleagues, than from being observed themselves. As such, schemes which involve teachers observing each other have been particularly successful in stimulating teachers' thinking about their own teaching.

Getting feedback from pupils. You can get useful feedback from pupils in a number of ways. You could ask pupils to write a diary about your lessons. In some cases this has been used to encourage pupils to reflect upon their learning experiences linked to a personal and social education programme or records of achievement. You could ask pupils to complete a questionnaire about your lessons, which explores aspects of your teaching and their experience of learning. You could interview pupils individually, or in groups, or hold a class discussion. Studies which have looked at teachers' use of feedback from pupils to evaluate their teaching, have invariably found that such feedback is very valuable and of high quality, and that the main reluctance by many teachers to solicit such feedback seems to be more to do with a fear that it may undermine the authority inherent in their role rather than concerns about its quality (see McKelvey and Kyriacou, 1985).

Many teachers have made use of a mixture of methods for data collection, and once you have focused more clearly on the particular aspect of your classroom teaching you wish to explore, the data collection can be made sharper and more specific. For example, Groarke (Groarke *et al*, 1986) described how, as a teacher of a fourth year junior school class, he used a diary, observations and an audiotape to explore how well pupils in groups set about various tasks. As a result, he noticed that because he organised the learning activities so that pupils had to complete an English or mathematics task before they could move on to 'more exciting' tasks, such as art or project work, some pupils simply rushed the first task. Furthermore, pupils with difficulties tended to become frustrated because they could not finish the first task in good time. He then introduced a rotating timetable in which the first task lasted a specified length of time. This relieved the pressure on pupils, and on him, and the new organisation of the activities led to an improvement in the quality of the work produced and in the pupils' attitude and motivation towards the work.

Ideas for reflection

A number of writers have produced texts aimed at helping teachers to reflect upon some aspect of their classroom practice by carrying out practical activities that will provide some useful data with which to analyse their teaching. For example, Pollard and Tann (1987) describe a number of practical activities that primary school teachers can use to address specific issues, such as the following:

- to 'measure' overall classroom climate at a particular moment in time
- to identify the overt and tacit content of classroom rules
- to gather information on how children feel about curricular activities which they undertake in school
- to evaluate an individual child's curricular experiences over one day or week
- to examine tasks in terms of their learning demands
- to investigate question-and-answer exchanges
- to evaluate different monitoring techniques
- to review the motivational qualities of a series of classroom activities
- to reflect on the quality and consequences of relationships between teacher and children over several weeks.

In addition, there are also some useful guides to exploring subject specific teaching. For example, Peck (1988) has described some activities which modern language teachers can use to analyse their own classroom practice by focusing on key aspects which differentiate between the styles and approaches used by different teachers, such as the degree to which the foreign language rather than English is used in the lesson, how and when the teacher intervenes, the emphasis on real communication, and the use of techniques such as modelling and fixing.

One other interesting development in schools has been the increasing use of the sharing of ideas and data about one's own teaching with colleagues, as part of a collaborative scheme in which teachers try to explore aspects of their own practice. Such schemes may involve a small group of teachers at a particular school, or a small group of teachers from different schools. Indeed, some in-service workshops for teachers are now based around the collecting and sharing of data about the development of their own practice during a specific period, lasting say one academic year, during which time each teacher focuses on and develops one particular aspect of their classroom teaching. Unlike traditional workshops, which tend to be one-off sessions involving inputs from 'experts', this approach means that the development is initiated, developed and sustained over a long enough period to have a significant impact on each teacher's practice. Furthermore, the approach also makes a positive use of the support and insight of colleagues on a regular basis engaged in the same enterprise.

Appraising a colleague

When you act as an appraiser, as part of a formal scheme of teacher appraisal operating at your school, it should take place in a context where the aims of the scheme are explicitly stated in its guidelines, together with details of the procedures to be followed concerning how and when you observe your colleague's teaching, and how your observations are to be recorded and reported. Such guidelines are likely to vary markedly from school to school, and certain details of the procedures may even operate differently to some extent within the same school.

The stages of teacher appraisal
Current practice indicates that the classroom observation element of teacher appraisal is likely to form part of a cycle of four key stages.

A pre-appraisal stage in which the teacher is asked to reflect upon their current classroom practice and areas of practice they may like to consider in detail or develop in some way (as well as reflection upon all other aspects of their work as a teacher to be included in the appraisal). This stage is most likely to make use of an open-ended questionnaire of some type.

Classroom observation based on prior discussion about which classes or lessons might be most appropriate to be observed, and whether the observer could usefully focus on any particular aspect of the teaching.

An appraisal interview in which the teacher's classroom practice and the identification of any development needs in this respect are discussed (as well as other aspects of the teacher's work).

Follow-up action in which issues and problems highlighted in the interview are taken further, as appropriate, particularly if it involves some degree of support to help the teacher carry out any agreed programme of development.

Your role as appraiser

In considering how best to carry out your role as appraiser in relation to the specific area of helping your colleague to reflect upon and develop their classroom teaching skills, a number of key issues are involved. First, your relationship with the colleague must be based on mutual trust and respect, you must have credibility with the teacher as someone whose observations and comments will be valued, and the exercise must be seen as collaborative (*viz* you are jointly helping each other to make the process as valuable as possible).

Second, you must be extremely careful and sensitive in how you communicate your feedback to your colleague. What you have to say must be scrupulously fair, and only judgemental in so far as you are raising an issue for discussion. The tone of the discussion should be one of equals comparing notes and views, and not one of you telling a colleague how to teach better. Third, it is essential that teachers being appraised feel they have ownership over the process. This means that you need to help your colleague reflect on their own practice and offer useful feedback to help them do so. Carrying out this role will require you to come to an understanding of the teacher's thoughts about their own teaching, their aims and intentions for a lesson, and their concerns about areas that might usefully be looked at in detail. The extent to which you convey this role may be limited by the nature of the scheme itself, and how far its emphasis is clearly formative or summative.

Recording the results of the appraisal

The report of the National Steering Group which looked at the six LEA teacher appraisal pilot schemes (DES, 1989c), includes the profile for recording the discussion about the teacher's classroom teaching presented in the ACAS report of 1986. This profile includes a section headed 'the teacher in the classroom', and comprises three elements, together with a prompt list for each.

Preparation. The activity was part of a properly planned programme; the aim of the activity was clear; a suitable approach was chosen from the options available; adequate and suitable resources were available; the learning environment had been considered.

Teaching skills. The material was well-presented; the pupils were actively involved; the teacher adapted the approach when necessary, was aware of individual needs within the group, and displayed mastery of the subject matter.

Follow-up. Homework is regularly set (if appropriate); pupils' work is marked and recorded regularly; pupils receive appropriate feedback about their work; parents are informed of pupils' work and progress in accordance with school policy; the teacher evaluates the success of his/her teaching.

This teacher appraisal profile contains a space next to each of these three elements to record a summary of discussion between the appraiser and appraisee. While a detailed listing of the major areas to be covered in an appraisal, together with their specific constituent elements, is helpful in indicating the aspects of teaching that may usefully receive attention, it becomes all too easy for the recording format to dictate what is looked at. As far as classroom teaching is concerned, the elements listed can take on a prescriptive quality and emphasize the summative aspect of appraisal. This will undermine the sense of ownership needed for the formative purpose to be encouraged. Fortunately, the experience of teacher appraisal schemes to date, including the six LEA teacher appraisal pilot schemes, indicates that a formative approach designed to encourage self-reflection and development has been widely employed (Cambridge Institute of Education, 1989; HMI, 1989).

Helping colleagues to develop their classroom teaching skills

In helping colleagues to develop their classroom teaching skills, it is often essential to go beyond simply giving advice and guidance. Your colleagues may need a variety of experiences and support in order to develop in a particular way. Most significantly, they may benefit from observing colleagues in their own school or teachers in other schools, or by taking part in workshops and courses for experienced teachers aimed at developing specific skills and expertise.

Changes in teaching, learning and assessment practices in schools have major implications for in-service training and resources. To expect teachers, for example, to be able to teach technology in the primary school, to prepare for coursework assessment activities in English, to use investigational approaches in teaching mathematics, clearly requires major training support for those teachers who are not confident or do not have sufficient current expertise in such approaches. Appraisal must not simply identify such needs, but should also plan for how such needs can best be met.

Managing your time

There are few jobs that can compare with teaching for the variety of demands you have to deal with: lesson planning, classroom teaching, marking, administration, dealing with pupils' personal problems, school-based decision-making, setting examinations, meeting parents, collaborating with colleagues, carrying out managerial responsibilities, helping new members of staff and student teachers, and the purchase of resources and equipment, such as textbooks, machinery and materials. Being able to cope with such demands efficiently and effectively will have a bearing, directly and indirectly, on the quality of teaching and learning that takes place in your lessons.

Effective time management

As such, you need to develop skills that enable you to manage your time and effort to best effect. In addition, because of the changing nature of your work as a teacher as a result of your own career development and changes in teaching generally, you will need to review and reflect regularly upon how well you are doing this.

Time management skills are essential to you managing your time and effort to best effect (Adair, 1982; Smith, 1988). Successful time management involves a number of important elements.

Be aware of your time.   You need to think about how much time you spend on particular demands, and decide whether this needs to be altered. For example, you may be spending too much time planning and preparing lessons, to the point where you are 'gilding the lily'. Analysis may reveal that you could reduce planning time without any noticeable loss of quality. You may also be able to improve on the efficiency of your planning by, for example, making greater use of lesson plans given previously or by planning a course of lessons at the same time rather than individually.

Prioritise.   You have to decide which order to undertake various tasks, taking account of their importance and urgency. The more important a task is, the more you should try to budget time to carry it out well in advance of any deadline, so that you do not have to do a rushed job under pressure at the last minute. If a task is urgent, you need to be flexible in postponing another task that can wait. The danger facing you is either always to try to meet demands simply in the order they confront you or in the order of their nearness to the point by which they must be carried out.

Plan your time.   You need to think about planning your time in the short-term (the school day), the medium-term (the school week), and the long-term (the academic term and year). Your planning for each time frame ought to reflect your prioritising, so that by the end of each period, the tasks with highest priority have been completed effectively, and those with lower priority slotted in as and when appropriate. Advance planning is helpful in enabling you to prepare in good time and make necessary arrangements or take on other commitments in the light of such planning.

Match time to tasks. Everyone has preferences about when and how they work most efficiently for given tasks. For example, some teachers may find marking work late during a weekday evening is particularly productive, while others may find using some time immediately after the end of a school day works better. Organising your time so that you can undertake particular tasks at your most efficient time for each can help you to develop regular routines that work well.

Deal with small tasks quickly. There are a number of tasks that can be dealt with in a short period of time, either immediately or at an early opportunity. Getting such tasks done and out of the way as soon as possible helps to keep your desk clear. Leaving them for later often results in your finding you have several rather small tasks needing to be done that begin to clutter up your planning, and their delay in completion may start to cause inconvenience to yourself and others. However, be alert to the fact that some such tasks, although small, may require more considered and careful attention, which you may need to think through or consult others about before acting.

Do not procrastinate. Once you have recognised that there is a task to be done, try to plan when you are going to carry it out, and then do so at that time. Much time can be wasted by thinking about starting a task on several occasions and each time deciding to leave it for no good reason, or because it involves some unpleasantness that you are inclined to put off.

Be realistic. You need to set yourself realistic demands, which means deciding what quality of work you can achieve in the time available. You may be trying to achieve too high a quality than is really required, or carrying out a task much sooner than necessary. Try not to accept unrealistic deadlines from others, as often such deadlines can easily be made more realistic.

Be able to say 'No'. Some teachers always say 'yes' when asked to undertake various tasks, and this can easily result in them becoming overloaded, and being the first to be approached when a new task needs to be allocated. Saying 'no' occasionally, provides others with feedback concerning how busy you may be and whether you feel the task is something you could usefully take on at the moment (this will help others in the school decide how best to manage the allocation to tasks to staff as a whole efficiently).

Delegate.   There are many tasks you can appropriately ask a colleague or a pupil to undertake, and from time to time you should review whether some of the tasks you carry out should be delegated. You could easily find yourself, for example, spending a whole day, off and on, trying to find out something about a pupil's circumstances that a colleague was better placed to have found out in just a few minutes. You may also be spending too much time on routine tasks, such as handing out books, equipment, worksheets, collecting marks and checking progress, in ways that can be better done by asking pupils to carry out some of these tasks.

As well as developing time management skills yourself, you should also be helping others to do so. For example, you should help pupils become aware of how to organise and pace their efforts in meeting deadlines within a lesson or over a longer period. In your dealings with colleagues, you can also help them to plan how tasks which effect you and others need to be organised so that appropriate deadlines and task allocations are set. For example, planning that pupils do not have too many coursework deadlines for the same time, or that time to mark examination work does not coincide unnecessarily with other busy periods in the school.

Time management skills are not a panacea that will alleviate all time pressures on you. Nevertheless, they do have a major impact on keeping avoidable pressures to a minimum, and helping you to maintain a high quality of performance in how you undertake the variety of tasks facing you. Indeed, they are one of the important sets of skills a new teacher needs to develop in the early years of teaching, and then needs to develop further as the nature of the demands facing you change as your role and commitments in school alter.

Dealing with stress

When teachers feel angry, depressed, anxious, nervous, frustrated or tense as a result of some aspect of their work as teachers, this is referred to as 'teacher stress'. Teacher stress has been widely discussed and re-searched for many years, and it appears that most teachers experience some stress from time to time, and that a sizeable number of teachers, about one in four, experience a great deal of stress fairly often (see Kyriacou, 1987, 1989).

Sources of teacher stress

The main sources of stress facing teachers fall into seven areas:

- pupils with poor attitudes and motivation towards their work
- pupils who misbehave and general class indiscipline
- rapid changes in curricular and organisational demands
- poor working conditions, including career prospects, facilities and resourcing
- time pressures
- conflicts with colleagues
- feeling undervalued by society.

How stress is triggered

The particular sources of stress experienced by individual teachers varies greatly from teacher to teacher. However, it does appear to be common that the experience of stress is triggered by the perception of threat to your self-esteem or well-being. This occurs in two ways.

First, and most often, it is triggered by you perceiving your circumstance as one where there are important demands needing to be met that you are finding difficult to do so adequately. The perception of threat is central to triggering the experience of stress here. If you do not see a situation as threatening, either because you feel you can meet the demands or because not doing so has little importance, stress does not occur. For example, if in the middle of a lesson, a pupil is rude to you, in a split second you may judge that you are not sure how to deal with the situation, and begin to feel nervous and anxious, particularly if you fear the situation may escalate. Furthermore, if your feel that if you fail to deal with the situation satisfactorily, you may be seen by the pupils, colleagues, or yourself as having inadequate skills in class control, this will threaten your self-esteem. Your feelings may be particularly strong if you regard the remark as an intolerable insult, which embarrasses you in front of the whole class. In such circumstances you will experience stress. In contrast, if you judge the situation as one you can deal with quite easily, and perhaps even as a rather trivial incident of little consequence, you will experience no stress.

The second way in which stress can be triggered is less obvious, but just as important. It is easy to see how difficulties in meeting demands, such as the example above, or tight deadlines for examining, meeting difficult parents, finding some apparatus is faulty just as a lesson has started, can elicit stress. However, stress can also be triggered in the absence of demands, as long as you perceive this circumstance as threatening your self-esteem or well-being in some way. For example, you may be hurt or upset to find you that have not be involved in some important school decision-making, or that a particular class or course you were hoping to teach has not been allocated to you. Again, if you perceive the circumstances as threatening your self-esteem, you will experience stress.

The impact of stress on your teaching

Teacher stress may undermine the quality of your teaching in two main ways. First, if you find teaching stressful over a long period, it may start to undermine your satisfaction with the work, and may lead to you becoming dissaffected with teaching. This is likely to have some impact on the time and effort you are prepared to give to the quality of your teaching. Second, when you feel stress, it can undermine the quality of your interaction with pupils in the classroom. Effective teaching very much depends on a positive classroom climate, and, in particular, on a good rapport with pupils, coupled with supporting and encouraging pupils' efforts. When you experience stress, that generosity of spirit towards pupils, which contributes to a positive classroom climate, can disappear, and you may react to problems and difficulties in a less well tempered, or even worse, openly hostile manner. As such, being able to deal effectively with stress will help you to maintain a high quality of teaching.

Coping strategies

Dealing with stress successfully involves using two types of coping strategies: 'direct action' techniques and 'palliative' techniques. In *direct action techniques*, you need to identify what is causing you stress and why, and then decide on a course of action that will deal successfully with that source of stress.

For example, if a particular pupil is disruptive almost every lesson, you may try a new strategy to deal with this. If you feel friction has developed between you and a colleague, you may try to re-establish a good relationship by being overtly more sociable and friendly towards your colleague. If you find that you are not able to mark pupils' work in good time, you may use some time management strategies to budget your time differently. As well as taking action on your own initiative, you can also usefully consult with colleagues to see if certain problems are common to them, or whether changes involving colleagues can help deal with the source of stress. The use of direct action techniques to deal with sources of stress may lead to immediate success, or may involve long-term action, particularly if successful action depends on you improving certain skills.

However, there are some sources of stress that you will not be able to deal with successfully by direct action techniques, and here you will need to be able to use *palliative techniques*. Palliative techniques refer to things you can do to relieve the experience of stress, even when the source of stress persists. Particularly useful are mental techniques, such as getting things in perspective, trying to see the humour in a situation, trying to detach yourself from personal and emotional involvement in a situation, and sharing your worries and concerns with others. In addition, physical techniques, such as trying to relax whenever possible, or having a coffee and social conversation with colleagues during a break period, are useful. Some teachers have developed useful techniques based on relaxation exercises that can help them to keep calm in a stressful situation. Relaxing after work is also very important.

Developing your own approach to coping with stress

In general, direct action techniques should almost always be tried to deal with a particular source of stress before palliative techniques are used, since if the former are successful, the source of stress is dealt with rather than accommodated. Your approach to stress, however, needs to be tailored to your circumstances and personality. For example, while for one teacher more preparation time at home would be helpful, for another more time spent at home relaxing would be better.

Take time to relax and unwind after work

Nevertheless, the following advice is useful (Cole and Walker, 1989; Gray and Freeman, 1988):

- identify and deal with problems as soon as possible
- develop skills and procedures to help you deal with the demands on you, particularly organisational and time management skills
- see whether some sources of stress are partly of your own making, such as avoidable confrontations with pupils or colleagues, or accepting tasks which are too taxing
- keep things in perspective, and try to form realistic expectations about your own performance and that of others
- share your worries and concerns with others
- maintain a balance between your work as a teacher and your life outside school (a healthy and enjoyable life outside school will enhance your self-esteem and the inner strength you have to deal with problems at school).

It is also important to note that teachers collectively can do much to mitigate stress by establishing a supportive climate in the school to help each other overcome difficulties, and by ensuring that demands on teachers are organised and allocated in a way that does not create stress which could have been avoided, such as allocating too many important tasks to the same member of staff, or fixing important deadlines too near to each other.

Key questions about your reflection and evaluation

1 *Do I regularly consider my current practice with a view to identifying aspects that can be usefully developed?*

2 *Do I make adequate use of evaluating my lessons in informing my future planning and practice?*

3 *Do I make use of systematic methods of collecting data about my current practice that may be helpful?*

4 *Do I try to keep well-informed about developments in teaching, learning and assessment in schools that have implications for my teaching?*

5 *Do I make use of a variety of different ways of developing a particular teaching skill (eg attending workshops, using training manuals, collaborating with colleagues)?*

6 *Do I make the best use of my involvement in a scheme of teacher appraisal to consider my development needs?*

7 *How well do I help colleagues to appraise and develop their classroom practice?*

8 *Do I regularly review how I can organise my time and effort to better effect?*

9 *Do I use a range of useful strategies and techniques to deal with sources of stress effectively?*

10 *Do I help create a supportive climate in my school to help colleagues discuss and overcome problems?*

Bibliography

Adair, J. (1982) *Effective Time Management*. London: Pan Books.

Angulo, L. M. V. (1988) An exploration of teachers' mental processes. *Teaching and Teacher Education*, 4, 231–46.

Assessment of Performance Unit (APU) (1989) *Communicating Mathematical Ideas*. London: HMSO.

Bennett, N., Desforges, C., Cockburn, A. and Wilkinson, B. (1984) *The Quality of Pupil Learning Experiences*. London: Erlbaum.

Berliner, D. C. (1987) Ways of thinking about students and classrooms by more and less experienced teachers. In: Calderhead, J. (ed.) *Exploring Teachers' Thinking*. London: Cassell.

Bowers, A. (1986) Interpersonal skills and conflict management. In: Tattum, D. P. (ed.) *Management of Disruptive Pupil Behaviour in Schools*. Chichester: Wiley.

Branwhite, T. (1988) The PASS survey: school-based preferences of 500+ adolescent consumers. *Educational Studies*, 14, 165–76.

Brown, G. A. and Armstrong, S. (1984) Explaining and explanations. In: Wragg, E. C. (ed.) *Classroom Teaching Skills*. London: Croom Helm.

Brown, G. A. and Edmondson, R. (1984) Asking questions. In: Wragg, E. C. (ed.) *Classroom Teaching Skills*. London: Croom Helm.

Brown, R. (1987) Pictures in the early years of schooling. DPhil thesis, University of York.

Calderhead, J. (1984) *Teachers' Classroom Decision-Making*. London: Holt.

Calderhead, J. (1986) A cognitive perspective on teaching skills. Paper presented at the British Psychological Society Education Section Annual Conference, Nottingham.

Calderhead, J. (1989) Reflective teaching and teacher education. *Teaching and Teacher Education*, 5, 43–51.

Cambridge Institute of Education (1989) *Report on the Evaluation of the School Teacher Appraisal Pilot Study*. Cambridge: Cambridge Institute of Education.

Child, D. (1986) *Applications of Psychology for the Teacher*. London: Holt.

Clark, C. M. and Peterson, P. L. (1986) Teachers' thought processes. In: Wittrock, M. C. (ed.) *Handbook of Research on Teaching* (3rd edition). New York: Macmillan.

Clark, C. M. and Yinger, R. J. (1987) Teacher planning. In: Calderhead, J. (ed.) *Exploring Teachers' Thinking*. London: Cassell.

Cole, M. and Walker, S. (eds.) (1989) *Teaching and Stress*. Milton Keynes: Open University Press.

Crooks, T. J. (1988) The impact of classroom evaluation practices on students. *Review of Educational Research*, 58, 438–81.

Cruickshank, D. R. and Kennedy, J. J. (1986) Teacher clarity. *Teaching and Teacher Education*, 2, 43–67.

Denscombe, M. (1980) Keeping 'em quiet: the significance of noise for the practical activity of teaching. In: Woods, P. (ed.) *Teacher Strategies*. London: Croom Helm.

Department of Education and Science (DES) (1988a) *National Curriculum Task Group on Assessment and Testing: A Report*. (The TGAT Report.) London: HMSO.

Department of Education and Science (DES) (1988b) *Records of Achievement: Report of the National Evaluation of Pilot Schemes*. (The PRAISE Report.) London: HMSO.

Department of Education and Science (DES) (1989a) *Discipline in Schools*. (The Elton Report.) London: HMSO.

Department of Education and Science (DES) (1989b) Initial teacher training: approval of courses. *DES Circular*, 24/89. London: DES.

Department of Education and Science (DES) (1989c) *School Teacher Appraisal: A National Framework*. London: HMSO.

Desforges, C. (1989) *Testing and Assessment*. London: Cassell.

Fitz-Gibbon, C. T. (1988) Peer tutoring as a teaching strategy. *Educational Management and Administration*, 16, 217–29.

Goacher, B. and Reid, M. I. (1983) *School Reports to Parents*. Windsor: NFER-Nelson.

Good, T. L. and Brophy, J. E. (1987) *Looking in Classrooms* (4th edition). New York: Harper and Row.

Grace, G. (1984) Headteachers' judgements of teacher competence. In: Broadfoot, P. (ed.) *Selection, Certification and Control*. Lewes: Falmer Press.

Gray, H. and Freeman, A. (1988) *Teaching Without Stress*. London: Chapman.

Groarke, J., Ovens, P. and Hargreaves, M. (1986) Towards a more open classroom. In: Hustler, D., Cassidy, A. and Cuff, E. C. (eds.) *Action Research in Classrooms and Schools*. London: Allen and Unwin.

Hanko, G. (1985) *Special Needs in Ordinary Classrooms*. Oxford: Blackwell.

Hargreaves, D. H. (1982) *The Challenge for the Comprehensive School*. London: Routledge and Kegan Paul.

Her Majesty's Inspectorate (HMI) (1985) *Education Observed 3: Good Teachers*. London: DES.

Her Majesty's Inspectorate (HMI) (1987) *Education Observed 5: Good Behaviour and Discipline in Schools*. London: DES.

Her Majesty's Inspectorate (HMI) (1988a) *Secondary Schools: An Appraisal by HMI.* London: HMSO.

Her Majesty's Inspectorate (HMI) (1988b) *The New Teacher in School.* London: HMSO.

Her Majesty's Inspectorate (HMI) (1989) *Developments in the Appraisal of Teachers.* London: DES.

Her Majesty's Inspectorate (HMI) (1990) *Standards in Education 1988–89.* London: DES.

Hustler, D., Cassidy, A. and Cuff, E. C. (eds.) (1986). *Action Research in Classrooms and Schools.* London: Allen and Unwin.

Johnstone, M. and Munn, P. (1987) *Discipline in Schools.* (Practitioner minipaper No. 1.) Edinburgh: Scottish Council for Research in Education.

Kerry, T. (1982) *Effective Questioning.* London: Macmillan.

Kerry, T. (1984) Analysing the cognitive demand made by classroom tasks in mixed-ability classes. In: Wragg, E. C. (ed.) *Classroom Teaching Skills.* London: Croom Helm.

Kounin, J. S. (1970) *Discipline and Group Management in Classrooms.* New York: Krieger.

Kyriacou, C. (1986a) *Effective Teaching in Schools.* Oxford: Blackwell.

Kyriacou, C. (1986b) Sixth-formers' perceptions of the effective teacher of mathematics at 'O' level. *British Educational Research Journal,* 12, 137–44.

Kyriacou, C. (1987) Teacher stress and burnout: an international review. *Educational Research,* 29, 146–52.

Kyriacou, C. (1989) The nature and prevalence of teacher stress. In: Cole, M. and Walker, S. (eds.) *Teaching and Stress.* Milton Keynes: Open University Press.

Kyriacou, C. (1990) Heads of departments' perceptions of the teaching of mathematics in secondary schools. Manuscript prepared for publication.

Kyriacou, C. and McKelvey, J. (1985) An exploration of individual differences in 'effective' teaching. *Educational Review,* 37, 13–17.

Kyriacou, C. and Marshall, S. (1989) The nature of active learning in secondary schools. *Evaluation and Research in Education,* 3, 1–5.

Kyriacou, C. and Roe, H. (1988) Teachers' perceptions of pupils' behaviour problems at a comprehensive school. *British Educational Research Journal,* 14, 167–73.

Laslett, R. and Smith, C. (1984) *Effective Classroom Management.* London: Croom Helm.

Leinhardt, G. and Greeno, J. G. (1986) The cognitive skill of teaching. *Journal of Educational Psychology,* 78, 75–95.

McKelvey, J. and Kyriacou, C. (1985) Research on pupils as teacher evaluators. *Educational Studies,* 11, 25–31.

Maslow, A. H. (1970) *Motivation and Personality* (2nd edition). New York: Harper and Row.

Mason, K. (1989) Diagnostic assessment in mathematics (DAIM) project. In NFER (ed.) *Assessment and Learning: Papers Presented at the Members' Conference*. Slough: NFER.

Mortimore, P., Sammons, P., Stoll, L., Lewis, D. and Ecob, R. (1988) *School Matters: The Junior Years*. Wells: Open Books.

Peck, A. (1988) *Language Teachers at Work*. London: Prentice Hall.

Perrott, E. (1982) *Effective Teaching*. London: Longman.

Pollard, A. and Tann, S. (1987) *Reflective Teaching in the Primary School*. London: Cassell.

Pye, J. (1988) *Invisible Children*. Oxford: Oxford University Press.

Robertson, J. (1989) *Effective Classroom Control* (2nd edition). London: Hodder and Stoughton.

Rogers, C. R. (1983) *Freedom to Learn for the 80s*. Columbus, Ohio: Merrill.

Rogers, W. A. (1989) *Making a Discipline Plan*, Melbourne: Nelson.

Rutter, M., Maughan, B., Mortimore, P. and Ouston, J. (1979) *Fifteen Thousand Hours*. Wells: Open Books.

Selkirk, K. (ed.) (1988) *Assessment at 16*. London: Routledge.

Shulman, L. S. (1987) Knowledge and teaching: foundations of the new reform. *Harvard Educational Review*, 57, 1–22.

Smith, A. D. (1988) *Starting to Teach*. London: Kogan Page.

Suffolk Education Department (1987). *In the Light of Torches: Teacher Appraisal*. London: Industrial Society.

Tomlinson. P. and Smith, R. (1985) Training intelligently skilled teachers. In: Francis, H. (ed.) *Learning to Teach*. Lewes: Falmer Press.

Troman, G. (1989) Testing tensions: the politics of educational assessment. *British Educational Research Journal*, 15, 279–95.

Turner, G. and Clift, P. (1988) *Studies in Teacher Appraisal*. Lewes: Falmer Press.

Vonk, J. H. C. (1983) Problems of the beginning teacher. *European Journal of Teacher Education*, 6, 133–50.

Waterhouse, P. (1983) *Managing the Learning Process*. London: McGraw-Hill.

Weade, R. and Evertson, C. M. (1988) The construction of lessons in effective and less effective classrooms. *Teaching and Teacher Education*, 4, 189–213.

Weston, P. (1989) Turning them off or bringing them on?: assessment, motivation and learning. In: NFER (ed.) *Assessment and Learning: Papers Presented at the Members' Conference*. Slough: NFER.

Wheldall, K. and Glynn, T. (1989) *Effective Classroom Learning*. Oxford: Blackwell.

Whetton, C. (1989) The development of standard assessment tasks for seven years olds. In: NFER (ed.) *Assessment and Learning: Papers Presented at the Members' Conference.* Slough: NFER.

Whitty, G. (1990) Building the bridge: the surveyor's report. Paper presented at a conference entitled 'Building the bridge: profiling the student teacher', York.

Wragg, E. C. (ed.) (1984) *Classroom Teaching Skills.* London: Croom Helm.

Wragg, E. C. (1988) *Teacher Appraisal.* London: Macmillan.

Wragg, E. C. and Dooley, P. A. (1984) Classroom management during teaching practice. In: Wragg, E. C. (ed.) *Classroom Teaching Skills.* London: Croom Helm.

Wragg, E. C. and Wood, E. K. (1984) Teachers' first encounters with their classes. In: Wragg, E. C. (ed.) *Classroom Teaching Skills.* London: Croom Helm.

Yinger, R. J. (1986) Examining thought in action: a theoretical and methodological critique of research on interactive teaching. *Teaching and Teacher Education,* 2, 263–82.

Author index

Subject index